DESIRE AND DISTANCE

Cultural Memory
in
the
Present

Mieke Bal and Hent de Vries, Editors

DESIRE AND DISTANCE

Introduction to a Phenomenology of Perception

Renaud Barbaras

Translated by Paul B. Milan

STANFORD UNIVERSITY PRESS

STANFORD, CALIFORNIA 2006

Stanford University Press
Stanford, California

Desire and Distance was originally published in French
in 1999 under the title *Le désir et la distance:
Introduction à une phénoménologie de la perception*
© 1999, Librairie Philosophique J. Vrin.

This book has been published with the assistance of the
French Ministry of Culture—National Center for the Book.

Printed in the United States of America on acid-free,
archival-quality paper

Library of Congress Cataloging-in-Publication Data
Barbaras, Renaud.
  [Désir et la distance. English]
  Desire and distance : introduction to a phenomenology of
perception / Renaud Barbaras ; translated by Paul B. Milan.
      p.   cm.—(Cultural memory in the present)
  Includes bibliographical references and index.
  ISBN 0-8047-4644-3 (cloth : alk. paper)
  ISBN 0-8047-4645-1 (pbk. : alk. paper)
  1. Perception (Philosophy) 2. Phenomenology.
  I. Title. II. Series.
  B828.45.B3713 2006
  121.34—dc22   2005017334

Original Printing 2006
Last figure below indicates year of this printing:
15 14 13 12 11 10 09 08 07 06

Typeset by James P. Brommer in 11/13.5 Garamond

Contents

Acknowledgments

I would like to express my appreciation to Paul Milan and to Seattle University, whose commitment and support have been unwavering throughout this project. I would also like to give thanks to R. Maxime Marinoni and Marcus Brainerd, whose careful reading and many suggestions have contributed greatly to the quality of the translation. A special debt of gratitude is owed to Rose Zbiegien, whose assistance in preparing the manuscript has been invaluable. Finally, I would like to thank Librairie Philosophique J. Vrin and Stanford University Press for their encouragement.

DESIRE AND DISTANCE

Introduction: The Problem of Perception

The question of perception not only has a "technical" or "regional" scope, as we still often tend to think; it merges in reality with the ontological question in its simplest sense, namely as an inquiry into the meaning of the being of what is. In fact, if "perceiving is perceiving something," as Pradines[1] writes, perception is indeed what opens us up to what "there is" —in other words, to being understood in the sense of what is given to us originarily before any determination, as the basis and condition for any determinability; being first takes the form of "something," and it is therefore indisputable that an inquiry concerning being refers back to perception as originary access to it. It is true that traditionally, and up to Heidegger himself, this originarity is denied to perception. We can undoubtedly believe that it is on the level of sensory experience that something is given primitively, that every determination and every objectivation unfolds on a preexisting basis: that of the world given to us precisely through perceptual experience.

However, in this instance this would be a mere illusion of a reflection forgetful of itself, inasmuch as this relationship to the fact of the world that I judge as originary has itself, as a condition, the apprehension of a meaning that supposes in turn the contact of consciousness with itself. My encounter with the something would become lost in darkness if it were not underpinned by an activity that constitutes it by grasping its significance; in the words of Merleau-Ponty, "The brute and prior existence of the world I thought I found already there by opening my eyes is only the symbol of a being that is for itself as soon as it is because appearing, and therefore appearing to itself, is its whole being—that is the being we call mind."[2] However, to cling to this thesis—the true significance of which we must recognize—is to neglect the indisputable dimension of perceptual experience in the sense that, whatever its value of truth, it is unquestionably lived and, so to speak, *index sui*. Even if it is denounced after the fact as illusory, it can be denounced only *after the fact*, so that the reflection that brings forth a significant relationship at the heart of experience takes everything into account except the fact that the something is *given* to me and that this significant relationship was first ignorant of itself. Thus, in considering itself as the condition of the encounter with the given, reflection pulls the ladder out from underneath itself because it can denounce perception as dependent only after having relied on a perceptual experience in which the brute fact of the world was given to it. This is why, as Merleau-Ponty writes again: "The whole reflective analysis is not false, but still naïve, as long as it dissimulates from itself its own mainspring and as long as, in order to constitute the world, it is necessary to have a notion of the world as preconstituted—as long as the procedure is in principle delayed behind itself."[3]

The decision to bring the question of perception to the fore involves a decision regarding being itself and therefore already represents taking a position within ontology; in effect, it comes down to admitting that the only possible access to being is our experience itself, that it is exclusively in what we live that we can discover its transcendence. This is what Merleau-Ponty becomes aware of, and clearly better than anyone prior to him. We could say indeed that his entire work aims at understanding what he calls "the basic fact of metaphysics" that resides in "this double sense of the *cogito* . . . I am sure that there is being—on the condition that I do not seek another sort of being than being-for-me."[4] We find an echo of this, albeit simplified, in the first lines of the inaugural chapter of *The Visible and the Invisible*, entitled "The Perceptual Faith and Its Obscurity": "We see the things themselves; the world is what we see."[5] It is in and through our experience, primordially perceptual, that we are initiated into the thing itself, that is to say, into what there is; it is in the "immanence" of what we "live" that we find a path toward transcendence; the phenomenological return to the things themselves signifies ipso facto a return to perception. Moreover, this perspective itself makes reference to a Husserlian discovery that is thematized under the heading of "the universal a priori of correlation between the object of experience and its modes of givenness"—a fundamental discovery since, Husserl writes, "my life's work was dominated by this task of elaborating the a priori of correlation."[6] Every being is the index of a subjective system of correlation, which signifies that any person imaginable can access being as such only through subjective data; the absolute character of being, in the sense that it is what relies on itself, does not form an alternative with the fact that its modes of access are relative to a finite subject.

Nonetheless, taken literally, the decision to search for the meaning of being in the being-for-me is so general that it cannot characterize only the phenomenological method *sensu stricto*, and if it can be qualified as "phenomenological," it can be done so only in a nontechnical sense, a sense that in any case is not Husserlian but suits Descartes as well as Hegel. The access to being through the *cogito*, understood in its elementary sense, draws at the center of the history of philosophy a truly vast field, though one nevertheless determined, a field that constituted the conditions for the possible emergence of a phenomenology.

Now, it is striking to observe that many philosophical currents that claim a method of access to being on the basis of experience fall short in this regard and do not succeed in accounting for experience as access to exteriority, as opening to something; perception in this context is always reduced to something other than itself and remains in a way "not to be found."[7] The empiricist perspective, for example, begins with the decision to cling precisely to experience, to what is given as given. However, the determination of this given in terms of sensations (or of impressions, in Hume's terminology) presents difficulties that paradoxically exhibit a disrespect for the given—in other words, a subjection of experience to categories that do not derive from it. The concept of sensation is in fact characterized by the confusion between the subjective state and what is experienced in it, between experiencing and that of which there is an impression. From this point on, the sensation remains an atomic datum and, so to speak, dead insofar as by itself it is incapable of representing or presenting something.

Punctuality and nonmeaning go hand in hand; because sensation cannot open to something, it finds itself cut off from other sensations, and since it does not disappear behind the object it is unable to communicate with other sensory moments. The relationship to the object, which defines the perceptual moment itself, depends then on a construct based on an association. We could easily demonstrate that the relationship to the thing—that is, the function of the manifestation—cannot be explained if it is not in some way inscribed beforehand in sensation. A sensation can recall the other sensations with which it constitutes an object only if it is grasped in advance in the perspective of this object, as one of its moments; otherwise the selective and ordered character of association would remain incomprehensible. Association therefore becomes useless at the moment it becomes comprehensible; the associationist theory always presupposes what it purports to explain. Thus, despite the appearance of a proximity to the given, empiricism is as far as possible from it, and the sensation, which is supposed to represent the most concrete—which defines the very meaning of concrete—is in reality what is most abstract. In fact, the need for reduction from the complex to the simple, the empiricist formulation of the return to the things themselves, is compromised by the confusion between *logical* simplicity and *psychological* or *phenomenological* simplicity. The fact that sensation can be extracted as the simplest element because it is indivisible in the final analysis of the thing does not mean that our *experience* of the thing is originarily constituted by sensations; here appears the confusion between what counts as the object of experience and what counts as the experience of which it is the object. Sensation proves to be the most abstract concept because it confuses the basis of an experience of the thing with the elements of an analysis of the object. Determination of perception based on sensation is unacceptable because it rests on a fundamental confusion and ultimately becomes part of a circular argument: it describes the conditions of the experience of the object on the basis of the object of which it is the experience.

Empiricism creates a subsistent world and then conceives of experience in a naïve manner as the effect of this world's action on the senses, whence the characterization of experience in terms of sensations, whose punctuality and multiplicity are merely the consequence of an implicit spatialization of sensitivity, conceived of as a kind of "sensitive cover" spatialization that is related to the exteriority of the parts of the body subjected to the world's action. Empiricism certainly has the virtue of emphasizing the dimension of *presence* that characterizes perceptual experience and distinguishes it from a conceptual—indeed imaginative—representation, but it constructs this presence from present data, sensations, thus not allowing itself to restitute presence in its true sense as presence of something. We must conclude from this that the access to the *cogito* that places us in the presence of being is not self-evident and is compromised by its subjection to the logic of being, by the projection of the categories of being onto the experience that gives it. Husserl refers to this fascination for the object that closes us off to the access to its conditions of manifestation as the natural attitude.

The return to perceptual experience therefore requires a concerted effort, a method; the shortcomings of empiricism consist in its undoubtedly not having understood that access to the immediate is anything but immediate. Cartesian doubt, the first attempt at phenomenological reduction, is motivated precisely by the consciousness of our subjection to the world in the form of blind belief in the validity of our perceptual judgments. It involves therefore an undoing of our immediate link with what appears, in order to clarify the very conditions of its manifestation, which means, in Cartesian words, making a conversion by negating the existence of the world toward an unquestionable being, a being that then appears as the conditional possibility of any manifestation. This being is none other than the thinking subject that is the absolute identity of being and appearance, or consciousness: to appear means to be for—but also "in"—a consciousness conceived as immediate relation to self, as immanence. In other words, perception is not an event of the world but an act of the subject, an act by which the latter enters precisely into a relationship with this world.

Perception is not constituted by sensations that would be present to consciousness as a thing is present in the world; it constitutes the world by representing it to itself. This is tantamount to saying that the encounter with something would not be if an act were not to intersect with it, an act that apprehends its meaning. However, the famous analysis of the piece of wax—which serves to eradicate on its own terms the naïve conviction that the sensory experience that gives us exteriority is the very model of evidence—reveals a misunderstanding of properly perceptual experience. Indeed, in describing our immediate experience of the wax in the form of an enumeration of distinct sensory qualities, Descartes subscribes to the empiricist approach. He fails to recognize that the color (as with the odor, and so on) of the wax not only is "*its*" color but *is given* as such. In effect, far from being a closed datum and for all intents and purposes neutral, color represents the wax, presents it, or incarnates it; it implies something "waxy," so that it communicates at once with the other "sensory qualities," such that that the color foretells the softness of contact with it and the muted sound wax makes if we strike it, as well as the way it will react when it comes into contact with a flame. It follows that at the conclusion of this effective eidetic variation (that is, the exposure of the wax to fire) none of the sensory qualities supposed to constitute wax remain the same; hence the judgment of identity concerning wax can be based only on the apprehension of a "body," of "something extended, flexible, and mutable," an apprehension that, as we know, relies on an intellection, on the only faculty able to grasp the power of infinite variation that is a body. However, in defining the piece of wax as a body, Descartes confuses the perceived wax with the physical wax, the latter being quantifiable because it is devoid of sensory qualities. This confusion is present from the first description of the piece of wax; to separate sensory aspects of the object of which they are aspects is necessarily to conceive of the object as a reality that transcends its modes of appearing.

In other words, in separating each aspect from its ostensive function, Descartes excises the wax from its sensory incarnation. The empiricist's description of the wax's presence in terms of pure sensory multiplicity and the intellectualist determination of the wax as quantifiable object constitute two sides of the same decision. The lack of unity characterizing the felt wax is compensated for by the positing of a pure object, by an excess of unity; but this excess of unity is achieved at the cost of a lack of presence.[8] Thus when Descartes emphasizes the fact that every perception is perception of *something*, he observes the active dimension of apprehending a meaning that is inherent in it. However, he hypostatizes this perceptual meaning in objective signification (more exactly in physical ideality), thereby cutting it off from its sensory incarnation. The perceptual moment in the strict sense —presentation of a meaning in the sensory or incarnation of an object in partial aspects—is completely missed. It is replaced by the juxtaposition of an intellection and sensations that are ideas without datum, which have no value other than to indicate an external existence insofar as they are merely the expression of my incarnated existence—in other words, of the finitude of my experience.

Thus, in confusing perception with intellection, Descartes assumes in a sense the objectivist prejudice that underlies empiricism. He indeed recognizes the necessity of going beyond the naïve understanding of knowledge as the thing's action on me, which is to say as an intraworldly event, to the benefit of apprehending a meaning, but he does not go so far as to contest the determination of the world as an ensemble of objects; if the existence of the world is indeed considered doubtful, the fact that the subject of existence—what is susceptible to existing—must necessarily be a substance is never doubted. In Descartes's eyes, perceiving something signifies necessarily apprehending an objective meaning in the sense of what is ideally determinable, and the question of perception then becomes one of the faculty that gives us access to what is constant in an infinity of variations. Descartes goes beyond empiricism, which missed the objectual pole of which sensory presence is the manifestation, but at the price of a blindness vis-à-vis the constitutive sensory dimension of perceptual appearance, vis-à-vis this abyss that separates the perceived thing from the conceived thing. The fact that the perception of the wax indeed requires the grasp of a unitary pole does not mean that this perception must be reduced to an intellection. In a certain way, the entire difficulty of a philosophy of perception resides in this distance, in the requirement that one conceive of an identity that does not depend on a positing, that one account for a *sensory* unity that does not differ from the diversity of which it is the unity.

We see that although recognizing that being-for-me is the only possible access to being, and although assuming therefore what Merleau-Ponty calls the fundamental metaphysical fact, the traditions that were just evoked do not succeed in developing a concept of experience that satisfies the nature of the problem; in short, they do not succeed in conceiving of perception for itself. However, their failure is helpful in that it indicates what the requirements are for a true thinking of perception. It is a question of reconciling the two dimensions that are alternately sacrificed by the traditions evoked here: the tradition of *presence* (which distinguishes perception from just any idea) and the tradition of *thingness* (which distinguishes it from the sensed and situates it in continuity with the thought). The task of a philosophy of perception is to conceive of the conditions of a profound unity between matter and form, diversity and unity, receptivity and activity. We already suspect that such a unity, if it must be something more than a mixture or a dialectical synthesis—in other words, a *primitive* unity inasmuch as it involves our originary relationship to what is—will unsettle the categories on the basis of which it has been characterized up to this point. On the other hand, critical examination of the classical conceptions of perception shows that their impotence in the face of its specificity derives from their subjection to the presupposition of the objective world. They consider as self-evident the existence of a reality in itself, one constituted by definite objects, and the fact that the existence of such a world can be doubted changes nothing regarding the certainty that if something exists, it will exist as a self-sufficient and fully determinable reality. In any case, the failure of the philosophy of perception stems from a confusion between the laws of this appearing reality and those that govern its appearance. the latter are immediately reduced to the former. It follows that one can conceive of perception authentically only on the condition that one not engage in this confusion, and consequently that one suspend this spontaneous ontology in order precisely to return to what makes it possible, to the structure of appearance. The characteristic difficulty of a philosophy of perception is that, to grasp in the act the movement by which experience initiates us to being, we must as it were refuse this initiation; we must cease to adhere to what is self-evident.

Husserl's philosophy is unquestionably the first that fully gauged the demands of a philosophy of perception and placed them at the center of its thinking. This is why we contend that there can be a philosophy of perception only as a phenomenology of perception. To understand the meaning of perception in Husserl's work, we must situate it at the center of a sort of typology of acts that constitutes the general framework put in place at the time of the *Logical Investigations*, at the center of which static phenomenology will completely unfold. Beyond the specific determination of psychic phenomena as intentional, Husserl borrows from Brentano a second characterization that Brentano himself, quoted by Husserl, formulates this way: "they are either presentations or founded upon presentations,"[9] which signifies that "nothing can be judged about, nothing can likewise be desired, nothing can be hoped or feared, if it is not presented."[10] What is significant here is the affirmation that a relationship not representative of the object— for example, an affective or volitional object—cannot be direct, cannot possess a type of object in the broadest sense that would correspond to it characteristically and be constituted in this relationship. In other words, there is givenness of object only in a theoretical sense, so that a nontheoretical relationship must be supported by a preexisting object constituted in a representation. The object of desire is not constituted in desire; it must first be constituted as an object in order to be desired. After a long discussion, Husserl takes up this thesis again for his own purposes and formulates it quite clearly: "An intentional experience only gains objective reference by incorporating an experienced act of presentation in itself, through which *the object is presented to it.* The object would be nothing to consciousness if consciousness did not set it before itself as an object, and if it did not further permit the object to become an object of feeling, of desire, etc."[11]

Whence the current topical distinction between objectivating acts and nonobjectivating acts that are founded on the former. It is undoubtedly in Husserl's Sixth Logical Investigation that we find the most complete definition of the objectivating act, a genus of which perception is a species: "We may say of this class of acts which alone concerns us here, *that in them unity of fulfilment has the character of unity of identification,* possibly the narrower character of *a unity of knowing*, i.e., of an act to which objective identity is the corresponding correlate."[12]

Thus the objectivating act sets us in relationship with a determined object, whether this object is or is not, strictly speaking, a cognitive object—in other words, whether it is effectively present or not. It should be pointed out that this weighty decision, which appears at first glance to be hardly questionable, commits the phenomenology of perception to a move in a direction that will prove—as is shown in what follows—fatal, so to speak. Does not defining perception right away as an objectivating act subject it in advance to conditions and categories of knowledge, thereby compromising the very possibility of considering its specificity? Does it not, at the same time, prevent us from accounting for its constitutive character—the access to an authentic transcendence? What is put into question here is the pseudo-evidence that any perception is perception of object. Moreover, to take these difficulties seriously implies understanding perception as a nonobjectivating act, which leads purely and simply to inverting the foundational relationship established by Husserl and, simultaneously, to finding oneself confronted by the difficult problem of the possibility of knowledge and objectivation on the basis of an originary givenness that is not oriented toward the object.

The division of acts within the category of objectivating acts is in a way required by their cognitive finality. Since the function of each is to refer to the object, the acts will be ordered according to their more or less effective aptitude for adequately presenting this object. The fundamental distinction in this regard, a distinction that Husserl advances in the First Logical Investigation and to which he devotes a significant part of the Sixth, separates signitive acts from intuitive acts, which include both imagination and perception. The former focus on the object "emptily"; they "conceive" of it without anything from the object being present in them. Husserl grasps them by means of the privileged example of the linguistic expression that refers to the object as absent. The latter are fulfilling acts in that they bring forth something of the object that was only focused upon, which they render present. As Husserl writes:

A signitive intention merely points to its object, an intuitive intention gives it "presence," in the pregnant sense of the word, it imports something of the fulness of the object itself. However far an imaginative presentation may lag behind its object, it has many features in common with it, more than that, it is "like" this object, depicts it, makes it "really present" to us. A signitive presentation, however, does not present analogically, it is "in reality" no "presentation," in it nothing of the object comes to life.[13]

It should be remarked that this relation of emptiness and fulfillment possesses a dynamic importance that corresponds to the fundamental orientation of intentionality toward knowledge. To say in effect that the signitive act focuses on emptiness is to say that it refers already to the object but in the mode of emptiness. As Levinas has shown, the signitive act does not involve a kind of mental image that would be equivalent to the object, as opposed to direct contact that characterizes intuition; he focuses on the object itself. Thus, as a test for a determined absence the signitive intention tends necessarily toward fulfillment; it opens the horizon of a givenness in fullness. Empty intentionality does indeed have the character of a lacking, and as a consequence intuition possesses an element of satisfaction; it "fills." Indeed, as Husserl writes:

To every intuitive intention there pertains, in the sense of an ideal possibility, a signitive intention precisely accommodated to its material. This unity of identification necessarily has the character of a unity of fulfilment, in which the intuitive, not the signitive member, has the character of being the fulfiller, and so also, in the most authentic sense, the *giver* of fulness.

We only express the sense of this last statement in a different way if we say that signitive intentions are in themselves "*empty*," and that they "are in *need* of fulness."[14]

It is appropriate however, to distinguish at the heart of intuitive acts between imagination that achieves the object only in image (thus representing it) and perception that reaches the object itself (thus presenting it). In perception we are concerned with the object "in flesh and blood" (*Leibhaft*) or in person; in fullness, Husserl says, "our experience is represented by the words: 'This is the thing *itself.*'"[15] Henceforth, perception is defined by Husserl as "originary giving intuition" because "to have something real given originarily and 'attentively to perceive' and 'experience' it in an intuiting simpliciter are one and the same."[16] Moreover, to the extent that knowledge is a search for adequacy, originary giving intuition (insofar as it places the object in presence) is a "legitimizing source of cognition"; such is the tenor of what Husserl does not hesitate to call "the principle of all principles."[17]

We see that, in Husserl's work, perception acquires a primordial status since, in affirming that it is an originary giving intuition, he indicates that it provides us access to being itself; perceiving is being put in presence of what is, and the only way of attaining what is in person is to perceive it. To be authenticated as being and to be perceived are reciprocal. It follows that any inquiry into being must pass through an inquiry into perception, that the sense of being of what is can be attained only in an eidetic of perception. Moreover, beyond the fact that it places perceptual experience at the center of phenomenology, this characterization of perception profoundly renews its meaning. In effect, insofar as it is defined as the fulfillment of a signitive focus, as presence "in the flesh," perception comes to exceed the level of empirical perception—strictly speaking, sensory perception. In other words, "The essential homogeneity of the function of fulfillment, as of all the ideal relationships necessarily bound up with it, obliges us to give the name 'perception' to each fulfilling act of confirmatory self-presentation . . . of '*object*.'"[18]

To the extent that the category, as well as an *eidos*, can be presented in themselves, we must speak of perception with regard to the act that attains them. Perception appears clearly in this context as a specific mode of intuition, one that places us in the presence of the thing itself (and not only of its image), and it can, in this regard, encompass intellectual intuition. Nevertheless, categorial intuitions remain founded acts in that they are necessarily supported by a sensory individual and that the fullness of categorial intuition derives from the individual's intuition. The originary meaning of perception refers indeed to the intuition of an empirical individual, and it is by extending the type of evidence that comes to light in sensory perception that we can speak of perception with regard to accessing a category.

This explains why, when it involves categorial intuition, Husserl speaks of perception "in a larger sense"; he distinguishes thematically between a narrow or *sensory* concept of perception and a broad or *suprasensory* concept. This broadening of perception is extremely significant even if it does not concern us directly for the moment. In fact, it opens the way to a definition of perception detached from any reference to sensory data. For Husserl it is indeed the sensory moment that ensures the dimension of presence in the flesh that distinguishes it from the perception proper to imagination; to speak of a thing as it is there in person, or "corporeally present," is to say that I sense it, that it manifests itself through sensory aspects. The ultimate fulfillment, which defines originary givenness, is ensured by the datum of sensation.[19] The fact remains that the definition of perception does not rely on sensation, and this is why the perceived escapes the prejudicial cut from the sensory and the suprasensory; to be perceived is to be present in person. In other words, it is to fill a deficient aim, and it is only because the sensory dimension ensures the full presence of the object, inscribes it spatiotemporally, and realizes as it were an optimum of presence that it can come to characterize perception.

In contradistinction to the whole tradition—which merges both perceived and sensed, whether this be to identify them purely and simply or to bring forth after the fact the presence of an intellectual activity at the center of perception—Husserl succeeds in characterizing the perceived in an autonomous way instead of reducing it to the sensed, all the while integrating and in a way justifying the constitutive character of the sensory dimension. The richness of this approach to perception is to my mind considerable, even if it is not certain that Husserl took full advantage of it. In effect, to the extent that perception is essentially sensory even while being defined other than by pure-and-simple merging with sensation, it will be possible to redefine the sensory in the light of perception, particularly to go beyond the naïve and abstract idea of sensation as atomic datum. On the other hand, the presence in the flesh to which perception is reduced is itself conceived of as the fulfillment of a preliminary intentionality; the ultimate status of perception therefore depends on the nature of this fulfillment, which is to say on the nature of the relationship between emptiness and fullness. If it were to turn out that this structural relationship between emptiness and fullness refers to a deeper mode of being instead of being reduced to the presence or the absence of the definite object, the characterization of the perceived would be profoundly shaken by it.

If it is true that perception attains the thing itself by virtue of its being an intuition, it is nevertheless distinct from an adequate knowledge; the perceived presents what was aimed at only as empty but does not present it integrally and therefore does not succeed in filling this aim fully. Husserl indicates this at the outset in the paragraph of the Sixth Logical Investigation that is specifically dedicated to perceptual fulfillment:

Perception, so far as it claims to give us the object "itself," really claims thereby to be no mere intention, but an act, which may indeed be capable of offering fulfilment to other acts, but which itself requires no further fulfilment. But generally, and in all cases of "external" perception, this remains a mere pretension. The object is not actually given, it is not given wholly and entirely as that which it itself is.[20]

Thus the fact that the thing is given *itself* does signify that it is given *such as it is in itself*; but the fact that perception gives us the object in person does not imply that it is an exhaustion of it. On the contrary; it attains it only partially. It is this situation that Husserl thematizes in the theory of adumbrations, only suggested in the *Logical Investigations* but carefully developed in book 1 of *Ideas Pertaining to a Pure Phenomenology and to a Phenomenological Philosophy*. It should be added however, that this theory of adumbrations is the opposite of a theory since it does not go beyond a description of the perceived as it is given "without ever going beyond the limits in which it is given." The power of the Husserlian theory of perception stems from the fact that it is guided by intuition as the legitimizing source of knowledge, which is tantamount to saying that it attempts to understand perception from (and as) the manner in which the perceived is given. The revindication of intuition means in this context that thinking must take shape from contact with perception instead of imposing its own demands on the latter.

Take, for example, this table I am looking at. I can walk around it, approach it, walk away from it, touch it with my hand; I am always conscious of a single, identical table, of a thing that in itself remains unchanged. Such is the elementary situation that characterizes perception. In a way, there is nothing more to think about; yet this is undoubtedly what is most difficult to understand. In fact, although the perceived table is always given as the same, the perceptions of the table (such are at least the words Husserl used), as the positions of my body as well as the uses of my senses that these perceptions presuppose, do not cease to vary. A same moment of the thing therefore appears through a diversity of manifestations,[21] which Husserl calls adumbrations: "Of essential necessity there belongs to any 'all-sided', continuously, unitarily, and self-confirming experiential consciousness [*Erfahrungsbewußtsein*] of the same physical thing a multifarious system of continuous multiplicities of appearances and adumbrations in which all objective moments falling within perception with the characteristic of being themselves given "in person" are adumbrated by determined continuities."[22]

Each manifestation of the table is indeed a manifestation of the table; it is the table itself that is presented in each manifestation and not a sign nor an image. Nevertheless, this manifestation remains an adumbration in that the table is presented from a certain point of view, from a certain angle, and not at all integrally, so that this manifestation is inscribed in an infinite series of other possible manifestations. On the one hand, the manifestation is nothing more than the table it presents; it is completely presentation, the very presence of the thing. On the other hand, the table itself is not distinct from this manifestation in which it appears and is given as this very manifestation.

We find ourselves therefore in a strange situation since the manifestation presents an object that is none other than that in which it is presented; the manifestation is surpassed toward the object, but this surpassing gives rise to nothing more than another manifestation. Thus it disappears, being replaced by the object that is erased simultaneously by its manifestation; unveiling the object, it veils it, since the latter is never grasped as distinct from what reveals it. In short, the manifestation presents the object as what itself remains unpresentable. This is why Husserl can speak of adumbration. The adumbration already gives what it outlines; it presents it, but insofar as it is only an adumbration it sidesteps what is outlined and postpones the full manifestation of it; in the adumbration, the object is presented rigorously as what requires formulation, and it has no other tenor beyond the adumbration than this requirement itself. Thus in perception the adumbration and the adumbrated object, the manifestation and what appears, are affected by a double constitutive ambiguity. The adumbration is simultaneously itself and the object it presents; it is the identity of itself and its surpassing (in other words, its obliteration). As for the object, it is simultaneously present in the sense that it is attained in person and indefinitely absent in the sense that no series of adumbrations can exhaust the tenor of being; it is the identity of a coming to presence and a retreat into the unpresentable.

It must certainly be added that if the presence of an object relies on the self-obliteration of the adumbration, the presence of the adumbration as such has as a correlate the object's retreat. This is an extremely difficult situation to conceive of since each of the terms exists only as passage to its opposite. Thus if there is a difference between an adumbration and that of which it is the adumbration, it is by no means a difference between two terms, since it is only due to its very adumbration—in other words, due to perception—that something such as a term can appear. This difference therefore does not differ from the identity; the difference or the distance from the object vis-à-vis the adumbration is summed up in the consciousness that "something" is present in or with the manifestation.

Affirming that the perceived thing is adumbrated in the course of manifestations ("lived experiences," in Husserl's terms), Husserl conceives of perception as a synthesis of identification that, on the basis of concordant adumbrations, apprehends the object as one and the same. We are therefore confronted with a consciousness "of the *one* perceptual physical thing appearing ever more perfectly, from ever new sides, with an ever greater wealth of determinations." Moreover, Husserl adds, "the spatial thing is nothing other than an intentional unity which of essential necessity can be given only as the unity of such modes of appearance."[23] In other words, perception as givenness by adumbrations is characterized by ambiguity, or rather the cobelonging of the one and the many. The thing is adumbrated in a plurality of manifestations, but its unity does not refer to any positive datum beyond this diversity; it is a unity that is constituted directly within the diversity of which it is the unity and that is in truth nothing more than this diversity itself. The one and the many pass in this instance into one another; if the diversity of the adumbrations refers to a unity that orders it, this unity itself is born at the center of diversity and always leads back to it. The adumbrations are therefore given as the manifestation of a unity that is constituted only in them, as a theme that would exist only in the form of its own variations. The unification of the diversity of the adumbrations does not constitute an alternative to the diversification of the one—in other words, their multiplication. It follows that if the unity of the thing is constituted only in and through the diversity of the adumbrations, *this unity itself is only an adumbrated unity.* It is not only the thing but its unity that is adumbrated in the flux of the manifestations.

We must specify the status of this description in order to gauge its full scope. In this instance, this does not involve a description that accounts for how the spatial thing appears to us in fact; rather, it represents a thematization of an eidetic necessity: the way in which transcendent being appears to us gives its essence. As Husserl expresses it, "It is neither an accident of the own peculiar sense of the physical thing nor a contingency of 'our human constitution,' that 'our' perception can arrive at physical things themselves only through mere adumbrations of them. Rather is it evident and drawn from the essence of spatial physical things . . . that necessarily a being of that kind can be given in perception only through an adumbration."[24]

This eidetic determination is grasped by a difference with the being of the lived experience, of the *cogitatio,* directly given to itself and such that it is in itself, without distance or depth, characterized by the identity of being and appearance. There is thus an eidetic abyss between experience and reality. The distinct manner in which they appear expresses a radical difference with regard to their being. Assuming this thesis, Husserl breaks radically with the tradition of philosophers of perception, a tradition that recognizes implicitly the possibility, at least in principle, of access to the thing that would dispense with adumbrations and that therefore explains this specific mode of givenness by virtue of our finitude. We perceive the thing through a flux of manifestations, but God—the subject with absolutely perfect knowledge—would naturally perceive the thing in itself. Such a perspective transcends the eidetic difference between lived experience and the perceived; it acts as if there were only a single manner of existing and therefore a single adequate modality of access to existing. To affirm that God could attain the perceived thing directly is to blur the border between the transcendent and the immanent, between the adumbrated and what is adequately given. Above all, it means that one misses the primary eidetic characterization of the perceived as intuition.

In effect, to postulate the possibility of perception without adumbrations is to consider the adumbration as that which compromises the access to the thing itself instead of giving it presence; in short, it amounts to confusing it with a sign or an image. Moreover, in perception the thing is attained "in flesh and blood"; the adumbration gives access to the thing itself and not to its image. Thus the transgression of the eidetic difference between the lived and the perceived refers on a deeper level to the ignorance of the fact that "between *perception*, on the one hand, and *depictive-symbolic* or *signitive-symbolic objectivation*, on the other hand, there is an unbridgeable essential difference."[25] It is now easier to understand the scope of the distinction between signitive intentionality and intuitive intentionality: by conceiving of perception as givenness in the flesh, Husserl provides himself with the means of distinguishing between *manifestations* (through which the thing is given) and simple *appearances*. The adumbration is not the thing, but neither is it an appearance since it is the thing itself that it adumbrates. The whole difficulty, then, is to conceive of the place of manifestation, between the appearance that it is not and the thing itself of which it is *only* the manifestation. The difference between adumbration and appearance names the constitutive ambiguity of the adumbration, which is brought together with the appearance by its difference from the thing and differs from the latter equally by virtue of its power of presentation, which is to say, its identity with what it adumbrates.

Going beyond the classical distinction between thing and appearance, Husserl invites us to understand perception directly from a movement of adumbration in which the thing itself and the moment of manifestation never fall outside one another. However, to the extent that the division between the appearance and the thing is no more than the division between the subjective and the objective, a coherent conception of perception undoubtedly requires that we question this duality more radically than Husserl did. Be that as it may, the eidetic abyss that separates the signitive from the intuitive must be respected; to say that the adumbration attains the thing itself is equivalent to saying that the thing itself is *given only by adumbrations*, and this is true for God himself. In reality such an affirmation is hardly surprising; if the thing is indeed transcendent, it can be given only by retreating under the gaze to a distance that could not be the reverse of proximity. Perception of the thing itself and givenness by adumbrations do not constitute alternatives if we understand transcendence to be a mode of existing and not an obstructed immanence; a truly transcendent reality can be given itself only on the condition of not being entirely given. One might as well say that the finitude expressed in the perspective character of our perception is an aspect of being and not the testimony of our limitation.

It is clear that Husserl goes resolutely beyond the limits of classical approaches to perception and thus situates himself beyond the alternative between empiricism and intellectualism. Speaking of adumbration, he abandons the idea of closed sensory data out of which the object would be constructed. The adumbration is not a component of the object, but its manifestation; the datum is itself only insofar as it incarnates a form. Nevertheless, this recognition of the function of manifestation or apprehension inherent in perception does not lead Husserl to exploit for his purposes intellectual analyses that succeed in explaining the access to something only by sacrificing its sensory dimension. It is true that perception is access to the thing itself and not reception of data, but there is precisely access to the thing itself only in sensory adumbrations; to perceive the thing itself is to grasp it in the flesh. The capacity of perception to open upon a pole of identity is not achieved at the price of a degradation of sensory moments in appearances. Due to the double discovery of the difference between empty intentionality and fulfillment on the one hand and of givenness by adumbrations on the other, Husserl succeeds—and undoubtedly he is the first philosopher to do so—in subscribing to the requirements of a philosophy of perception; in other words, he succeeds in conceiving of the conditions of an experience that initiates us into being. That is why a philosophy of perception must consider this perspective and why its primordial task must consist in assessing Husserl's insights in order to draw all the consequences from them. Indeed—and such is the guiding thesis, or rather the problematic that nourishes this work—the conceptual framework set forth by Husserl to establish and elaborate his theory of perception (at least in the context of static phenomenology) remains in the background vis-à-vis what the doctrine of adumbrations promises. Put differently, there is an undeniable tension between the descriptive moment of the theory of perception and the interpretive moment that carries out presuppositions to which the description actually stands in opposition. Even though he succeeds in establishing grounds for perception strictly speaking and therefore possesses the means to elaborate a conceptual framework that is his own, Husserl draws on categories that originate from a tradition that misunderstood the specificity of perceptual experience—whence a series of tensions, gradual evolutions, and displacements that ultimately lead him to compromise the project whose theory of adumbrations was so promising. Briefly, instead of sticking to perception just as it is given, he advances a thought that goes beyond the limits within which the perceived is given. The aim here is therefore to attempt to pursue what is suggested in this Husserlian doctrine of perception, at the very least to gauge the shocks that such a description cannot help but create within this field of philosophy and in its most fundamental categories—in short, to take the first steps toward a philosophy of perception. However, in this context it must be understood in a renewed sense. It does not in fact involve approaching perception as one segment of being among others regarding which our philosophical instruments could again be put to work. It involves reforging our instruments by testing the singularity of perception.

It seems in fact (and this becomes clearer in what follows) that the philosophical tradition was constituted on the basis of a fundamental experience or an astonishment that leaves no room for the specificity of perceptual experience and in which it was ultimately concealed. The task of a philosophy of perception is therefore not to attempt to appropriate perception by means of categories at its disposal but to allow itself to be reformed through contact with perception; it must not conceive of perception so much as conceive *according to* it. Moreover, if it is true that Husserl did not succeed in avoiding the recourse to a conceptual framework that remains awkward vis-à-vis its object, such an undertaking must begin by attempting to elucidate the presuppositions that underlie Husserl's analysis.

1

A Critique of Transcendental Phenomenology

Husserl's analysis of perception allows us to elucidate the structure of *appearance* as such. It draws our attention to the very phenomenality of phenomena and to its own modalities; in this regard, it is based on a phenomenology in a radical sense of the word. This structure of appearance is most often ignored, by virtue of its ostensive function; in effect, in disappearing behind the object, in making it present, the adumbration is dissimulated as specific moment and as such causes itself to be forgotten. Naïve consciousness becomes fascinated by the appearing, captured by its presence—which it tends spontaneously to split from its appearance, in other words, to posit as self-sufficient—such that the moment of manifestation, the adumbration, is reinterpreted according to the realist mode as a "subjective appearance," as the effect of a real thing on a consciousness that is itself real. The task of the phenomenological *épochè* is precisely to break this fascination in order to revert from the appearing to its appearance—in short, to suspend the thesis of existence characteristic of the naïve or natural attitude. For this reason, insofar as it is the nature of phenomenality to conceal itself in what it presents, it would not be inaccurate to say that the aim of phenomenology is to show phenomenality, to render appearance as appearing. The whole difficulty, which makes the *épochè* a particular form of vigilance rather than a unique gesture acquired once and for all, consists in clinging to the structure of appearance as such, in not using surreptitiously during its description characteristics belonging to the appearing being whose appearance is the condition of possibility. The rigor of a phenomenology of perception therefore depends on its ability to cling rigorously to appearance as such, to respect its autonomy, so that the *épiché* could ultimately be defined as the prohibition against importing or transferring within appearance any determination stemming from the appearing.

In accordance with this first description of perception, phenomenality can be characterized as the originary cobelonging, the mutual interweaving between manifestation and appearing. The adumbration puts us in the presence of the thing itself, its being consisting in a presentation. The appearing being, by contrast, is given as being "there," in person, but this being has no content other than the ensemble of the manifestations that initiate in it and never falls outside its moments of manifestation. It is this situation that Merleau-Ponty thematizes under the title "perceptual faith": the world is nothing *more* than what we perceive, and yet we perceive the world *itself*. Manifestation is its own surpassing; it is more vast than itself, since it is the unfolding of the appearing. The appearing, for its part, remains always at a distance from self because it appears only in disappearing from this in (and as) what it appears, only in being in a way more profound than itself. At issue here is an originary and perfectly singular mode of solidarity, since each of the terms is the unity of itself and its corresponding term; the structure of appearance thwarts the laws of formal ontology, which are only the laws of the appearing. The task of an authentic philosophy of perception therefore consists, while maintaining itself in the pure element of appearance, in qualifying and conceiving of this structure of phenomenality with respect to its originality. What exactly is the nature of manifestation? To *whom* does the appearing appear? What is the subject's sense of the being of the manifestation? Finally, *what* exactly appears? Does what appears and what constitutes the object of perception exist in the mode of the object? To approach the ensemble of these questions is to attempt to give a meaning to the concept of *intentionality*, which is both central and mysterious. Moreover, it seems to us that Husserl, at least before the genetic "turning point," cannot respond clearly to these questions because he does not succeed in remaining in the element of pure appearance; he tears the intentional fabric in keeping with the duality between the subjective and the objective, thus remaining on the margins of the system of *épiché* that he advocates.

In *Ideas I*, the analysis of perception appears as a necessary moment, subordinated to the unfolding of the thematic of phenomenological reduction. In effect, Husserl proposes an initial characterization of *épiché* as neutralization of the general thesis of the natural attitude; however, instead of implementing it immediately, he returns to the sphere of phenomenological psychology in order to develop an eidetic of consciousness and natural reality. This eidetic aims at underlining the contrast between the absolute being of the immanent (of the lived) and the contingent being of the transcendent (of the perceived) and thus aims at laying the groundwork for effective and definitive implementation of the *époché*. The latter passes through the hypothesis of the nonexistence of the world—as a hypothesis rendered possible by the eidetic characteristic of the transcendent—and opens upon a reduction to the region of pure consciousness, the originary region within which and from which every being draws its meaning.

In discovering the sphere of consciousness as residuum of the *époché*, Husserl thus justifies assimilation of phenomenology to a transcendental idealism. Therefore, the description of perception as givenness by adumbrations must be understood in its opposition to the determination of consciousness, of the lived experience, that appears right away as what is given by the phenomenological *époché*. In effect, "*What can remain, if the whole world [. . .] is excluded*,"[1] if not a region of original being constituted by pure lived experiences? The latter can be described in terms of their own "content," by virtue of an eidetic necessity; the essence of the *cogitatio* involves in effect "the essential possibility of a *reflective turning of regard* and naturally in the form of a new *cogitatio* that, in the manner proper to a *cogitatio* which simply seizes upon, is directed to it. In other words, any '*cogitatio*' can become the object of a so-called 'internal perception.'"[2] Moreover, in contradistinction to the transcendent thing, the characteristic of lived experience is that it is not given by adumbrations. Nothing in it exceeds its manifestation; it is nothing more than it appears, an absolute identity between appearing and manifestation. It should be emphasized that the capacity for becoming the object of an internal perception is based on this characteristic essence of the lived experience; it is because it exists in the mode of referring to itself, of appearing to itself, that it can be reflected upon.[3] We point out, on the other hand, that Husserl has recourse here to a concept of perception that is exemplary since the lived experience conceals neither any distance nor any emptiness; it fills perfectly the reflection that focuses upon it (or, in other words, fullness itself as a mode of existing). It can be seen here that there is a profound solidarity between the characterization of perception as fulfillment and the determination of the absolute as lived. It follows from this analysis that "every perception of something immanent necessarily guarantees the existence of its object"[4]; in short, it is unquestionable in contrast with the transcendent object that, by virtue of its adumbrated being, can always prove not to exist. On the basis of this opposition between the absolute being of consciousness and the contingent being of the transcendent, Husserl is then able to take the step of constituting the transcendent within transcendental consciousness.

It is therefore not surprising that Husserl neither sticks to his description of perception as givenness by adumbrations nor attempts to conceive of appearance on the basis of manifestations insofar as they are manifestations of things. On the contrary, he reinvests in a concept of appearance that lies at the heart of *Ideas I* and that alone can sustain the manifestation of a transcendence; to say of a reality that it appears is to say that it is apprehended in and by a *consciousness* and therefore that it is constituted by means of *lived experiences*. The appearance of the worldly appearing necessarily refers to a more originary sense of phenomenality, namely the manifestation of the lived experience to itself; to appear is either to be lived or to be constituted by means of lived experiences. From this flows the analysis that Husserl advances regarding the real composition of perception. The adumbrations "are included among '*the Data of sensations*'. . . . Furthermore, in a manner which we shall not describe here more precisely, the Data are animated by '*construings*' within the concrete unity of the perception and in the animation exercise the '*presentive function*,' or as united with the construings which animate them, they make up what we call '*appearings of*' color, shape, and so forth."[5] Thus the appearance of the qualitative or formal moments of the object, as well as the object itself, is composed of two types of lived experience. The first is the sensuous *hylé*, corresponding to pure datum of sensation prior to and independent of any grasp of a meaning and therefore of even any minimal objectivation. The *hylé* is the pure experiencing of what is grasped without distance, the moment of pure receptivity; it is felt and not perceived (such as, for example, a sound that sounds in me "before" being apprehended as the sound "of this violin"). This must be contrasted with the experiences that carry in them the specific property of intentionality; these lived experiences animate the hyletic data by apprehending them in accordance with a sense that confers on them an ostensive function—that constitutes them as manifestations of something. Husserl qualifies them as noetic because they form the specific element of the mind, which they breathe, so to speak, into sensations that of themselves are inert. It is therefore by means of the noesis that animates it that the *hylé* becomes the adumbration of the object's corresponding moment; the adumbration refers to an adumbrating that itself relies on the animation of a sensible content by a sensory intentionality. For this reason, it is necessary to be careful not to confuse the hyletic moment with the corresponding objectual or noematic moment:

> It must be borne clearly in mind that the Data of sensation which exercise the function of adumbrations of color, of smoothness, of shape, etc. (the function of "presentation") are, of essential necessity, entirely different from color simpliciter, smoothness simpliciter, shape simpliciter, and in short, from all kinds of moments belonging to *physical things*. . . . The adumbrating is a mental process. But a mental process is possible only as a mental process, and not as something spatial. However, the adumbrated is of essential necessity possible only as something spatial . . . and not possible as a mental process.[6]

Thus the relation between the one and the many is understood within perception. The diversity of manifestations does not contradict the identity of what appears because the adumbration and the adumbrated are situated on distinct levels. A sensible color (*Empfindungsfarbe*) can vary in the flux of the experience, all the while adumbrating a same noematic color or a same colored object; by noesis, the variations on the hyletic level will be constituted as changing manifestations of a single identical thing.[7] Thus the noematic moment is to the *hylé* what form is to matter, and it is this relation that finally allows us to reconcile the diversity of adumbrations with the unity of the appearing object; one and the same form can be incarnated in distinct matters. In the same way that matter is always matter for a form, the difference of the adumbration does not constitute an alternative with the unity that it forms with the object in the manifestation; for this reason Husserl insists on the fact that "this remarkable duality and this unity of *sensuous hylé* and *intentive morphé* play a dominant role in the whole phenomenological sphere."[8]

    In moving from the description to the analysis of perception—that is, in elucidating its "real composition"—does Husserl clarify perceptual appearance? Does he respect its specificity? Is the reconstitution of transcendental phenomenality from two types of lived experience being articulated in accordance with the relationship between matter and form a true reconstitution that restitutes the tenor of what it purports to explain? Are we not involved, rather, in a decomposition of the structure of appearance by which phenomenality is disfigured and ultimately lost in terms of what is specific to it? This reconstitution of appearance lacks its essence because it relies on an unwarranted displacement: the analysis unfolds on a basis on which something like a composition can be brought to light, but this occurs at the cost of an inability to rejoin the effective figure of appearance. This displacement consists in situating the analysis on the basis of lived experiences, conceived of as "contents" accessible in an adequate intuition, in being given a sense of being of the subjectivity that not only prevents accounting for appearance but also reactualizes presuppositions that all phenomenological analysis aims to uproot. Indeed, this displacement appears from the beginning of the outlines of the description; the intuition of givenness by adumbrations is immediately inscribed in a conceptual framework that tarnishes its brilliance.

In this regard, it is revealing to compare section 41 of *Ideas I*, which deals with the real composition of perception, with the opening pages of *The Visible and the Invisible*, which are dedicated to perceptual faith. Husserl offers an example: "Constantly seeing this table and meanwhile walking around it, changing my position in space in whatever way, I have continually the consciousness of this one identical table as factually existing 'in person' and remaining quite unchanged. The table-perception, however, is a continually changing one; it is a continuity of changing perceptions."[9] In the opening pages of *The Visible and the Invisible*, Merleau-Ponty attempts, just as Husserl does, to describe perception without presuppositions, to situate himself as close as possible to experience. The example chosen is still the one involving the table:

I must acknowledge that the table before me sustains a singular relation with my eyes and my body: I see it only if it is within their radius of action; above it there is the dark mass of my forehead, beneath it the more indecisive contour of my cheeks—both of these visible at the limit and capable of hiding the table, as if my vision of the world itself were formed from a certain point of the world. What is more, my movements and the movements of my eyes make the world vibrate—as one rocks a dolmen with one's finger without disturbing its fundamental solidity.[10]

In both cases, the example of the table involves showing a certain relativity of perception while simultaneously showing that it does not compromise the permanence of the appearing thing; yet this relativity assumes, in each of the two authors, a fundamentally different significance. Merleau-Ponty clings strictly to what we can say about perception. Perception assumes a body in that at least my bodily movements, indeed the very mass of my body, can hinder me from perceiving. My vision of the world is always accompanied by a perception of my body, visible at the limit and in its limits: it is covision of my body. This signifies that my vision is made from the midst of the world, always from a certain point of view, and that the manifestation of the world is relative to this worldly being. This relativity that causes me to grasp the vision as "mine" depends on the mobility of my body, both in totality and in certain of its parts. Thus the variation of manifestations, the movement that characterizes the flux of the adumbrations, refers to the strictly spatial movement of my body. Now, if my movements can induce a movement of the thing seen ("make the world vibrate"), I never attribute these movements to the world—as if my mobility were unfolding a bundle of appearances—and its "fundamental solidity" is not weakened by it; the variations of my body do not hinder me from having the conviction of accessing the world itself. It should be pointed out here that the invariant contrasting with the bodily movement is grasped as the world and not as a thing. Be that as it may, my vision of the table depends on a body and therefore always implies a perspective, so that the table is seen from different angles, in different ways. It can even happen that what I judged from one perspective to be a table turns out to be something else owing to a movement giving me a more favorable perspective. But in any case, what I see is given as being *there* in the world—endowed with an unshakeable solidity because with regard to its being it exists independently of its corporeal variations—even if *what* is there turns out to be different from what I believed it to be at first sight. Merleau-Ponty adds, a little further on, thereby clarifying the meaning (at least in a negative sense) of the description: "I would express what takes place badly indeed in saying that here a 'subjective component' or a 'corporeal constituent' comes to cover over the things themselves: it is not a matter of another layer or a veil that would have come to pose itself between them and me."[11]

This is, however, the position toward which Husserl's description is moving. Just as Merleau-Ponty does, he starts by taking into account my bodily movements, so as to conclude from this that "the perception of the table does not cease to vary." In other words, the change induced by the body's movements is interpreted not as a variation in aspect of the perceived thing but as a change in the perceptions themselves. Merleau-Ponty relates bodily movements to the world's solidity, but at most they make the world vibrate, thus leaving the manifestation on the side of what it causes to appear; Husserl separates manifestation in the form of perception from what appears through it and thus contrasts a series of changing perceptions with an object that does not change. The first part of the text confirms this: in spite of these changes, "I have continually the consciousness of this one and identical table, which *in itself* [my emphasis] remains unchanged." If the table that remains invariable is in itself, we must conclude from this that the perceptions that continually vary are of the order of the *for itself*. Thus whereas in Merleau-Ponty's description it is the same object that varies according to the body's movements and therefore remains the same throughout the variations in its aspects, for Husserl, by contrast, the object remains in itself the same while my perception is continuously varying. Moreover, as Granel writes:

When I walk around the table, it is always the table that I see, as the text has just said; but then we must also say that perception doesn't vary. Except for having decided to cut this living unity that the real and I create in perception in *two* elements, of which one would be the locus of the unity that does not vary, namely the object, and of which the other would be the locus of pure change, namely the subject.[12]

Strictly speaking, I perceive the same object from different aspects, so that it is not my perception that varies but the aspects according to which the object is given to it. By contrast, Husserl separates the manifestations that continuously vary from the object that is given in them (and that therefore becomes immediately qualified as in itself) in order to turn them into perceptions, something essentially subjective; he then finds himself forced to explain how a changing flux of subjective perceptions can give rise to an immutable object. Hence we can posit the hypothesis that in the final analysis this split refers to the impossibility of conceiving of an "object" that remains the same in its own variations, of reconciling *on the very level of the transcending* the variety of the aspects with the unity of what is adumbrated in them. Husserl's subjectivation of appearance would be thus rooted in a certain idea of the object that would impede it from integrating in it the infinite renewal of the adumbrations. From this point of view, it is significant that Merleau-Ponty moves from the perception of my table to the invariability of the world, while Husserl clings to the existence "of this one identical table."

In any case, the continuation of the two texts that we are contrasting largely confirms this interpretation. Husserl in fact adds: "I close my eyes. My other senses have no relation to the table. Now I have no perception of it. I open my eyes; and I have the perception again."[13] Unquestionably we are involved here in the hypothesis of the "subjective component" that Merleau-Ponty quickly excludes. Since the table that disappears when I close my eyes reappears the same when I open them, we must recognize that in reality the table does not disappear and therefore distinguish the table itself from my perception, which depends on the movements of my eyes. We must, though, still recognize that when I close my eyes I no longer have a relation to the table; I no longer have a perception of it. First of all, Husserl is obliged to introduce the abstract hypothesis that "through my other senses I have no relation to the table." As Granel points out once again, when I close my eyes "I still really have a perceptual relation to the table, in the sense that it is *to* the table that I have become blind. It is *to* it that I have closed my eyes; it is *from* it that I turn away."[14] At the very least, since it can happen that I close my eyes to the table while simply turning away from it, thus incidentally, without a deliberate act of the will motivated by a phenomenological experiment, it must be admitted that when I close my eyes (and all my other senses) to the table I still really have a perceptual relation to the world. I close my eyes to the table to better hear the noise that sounds outside, or perhaps, if I am satisfied with ceasing to look at it, I continue to perceive the world against the background of which I grasp it as a certain absence. The manner in which Merleau-Ponty pursues his description confirms this: "With each flutter of my eyelashes a curtain lowers and rises, though I do not think for an instant of imputing this eclipse to the things themselves; with each movement of my eyes that sweep the space before me the things suffer a brief torsion, which I also ascribe to myself."[15]

First of all, Merleau-Ponty mentions a constitutive "blindness" of my bodily relationship to the world: the flutter of my eyelashes. It could be shown that the clarity of the world's presence presupposes these continual little faintings, as if it were to reemerge at each instant from a phase of indetermination. The metaphor of the curtain reveals the meaning of this experience: when I close my eyes, it is neither the world that disappears nor my perception that vanishes; instead, *my perceptual relation to the world changes in character.* In being lowered on a scene, for example, the curtain indicates its presence; the world's scene is always perceived through the curtain of the eyes, always present. The second sentence formulates quite clearly the general situation of perception, even if it concerns the experience of mobility: "the things suffer a brief torsion, which I also ascribe to myself." When my body moves, the world changes aspect, but to the degree that I perceive conjointly my body's movement I also attribute this movement to myself. This is why, in changing aspect, the world is not shaken in its fundamental solidity. There is no such thing in this context as a subjective perception; description can recognize only a correlation between my movements and the manifestations of the world.

It appears therefore that the first descriptions Husserl proposes of perceptual appearance are not faithful to the very figure of the perceived because they are immediately dependent on an implicit displacement of appearance on the side of subjectivity, a displacement that is thematized throughout his entire work—a theory of lived experiences in which the perceived is constituted. More precisely, the descriptive distinction between changing perceptions and the perceived thing as immutable is echoed within the theory in the form of the distinction between hyletic datum and the corresponding moment of the noema. We can justify the manifestation's autonomy vis-à-vis the appearing only by supporting it on the basis of a moment that is *purely* subjective, that does not appear. Such is exactly the status of primary hyletic datum: it is a pure sensing, in which no distance is opened, in which no meaning is adumbrated; it is a movement that has no other function than to be the substratum for an apprehension.[16] It is indeed on the condition of positing a strictly immanent moment that is only sensed that we can support the manifestation's autonomy—perception's autonomy in relationship to the perceived. Moreover, we can hardly avoid thinking that in this instance it involves a construction, a retroactive projection of the noematic moment, of an already objectual aspect within a consciousness whose existence was previously postulated. The sensed would then be something perceived as separated from the object, a moment of manifestation artificially deprived of its ostensive value, of its being in the strictest sense. Can we conceive of a pure appearance that is not right away and of itself appearance of something? Can we distinguish, even legitimately, a red that would be only experienced and not spatial from a red as moment of object, that is to say, spatial? Can we conceive of a sensing that does not inscribe me in a world, as simple as it might be? Patočka, who exhibits a great deal of insight regarding these questions, writes the following: "When I find myself passively given to my sensations that, so to speak, submerge me, for example upon waking, before my lived experience assumes the shapes of things, isn't it a simple fog that appears to me, a chaos that doesn't resemble things in any way, but that has no less a character of object?"[17]

Thus there is no given that is not already an object, in the minimalist sense of the word according to which it appears there in the world and therefore is given as a moment or an aspect of this world, even if the latter is still undetermined, without identifiable things. There is no given that does not give rise to a perception. It is true that we must differentiate between things as such and moments on the basis of which they appear; the thing itself must be distinguished from its manifestation, which is dependent on the situation of the person who perceives as well as on the environment. In this sense, the Husserlian necessity of distinguishing an objective moment from a nonappearing moment on the basis of which the first appears is fully justified. However, what is much less justified is the determination of the mediating moment as purely subjective, foreign to all transcendence. As Patočka points out:

There is a difference between the characteristics that I attribute to the "thing itself" as its properties, and those that, although given in concert, do not belong to it, but with the aid of and on the basis of which it appears. However, the two species of characteristics appear in the world, in the phenomenal field "there in front of" me; they are not present as lived experiences, as something subjective.[18]

The red of this object is a moment of manifestation that disappears in front of the thing that it makes appear and in this respect is not perceived; it must be contrasted with the red on which I can focus as autonomous object. But the fact that the former is not perceived does not mean that it is "subjective" in the sense that Husserl understands it; it is a mediator, a moment of manifestation that, if it is not itself an object inasmuch as it corresponds instead to some part of the object that is dependent on its situation and on my orientation, it is nevertheless "objective" in the sense that it is grasped in the world, next to the thing that it causes to appear and therefore is perceptible. The difference then is not between the sensed and the perceived but between the perception of objective moments, of manifestations as such, and that of the object "itself." Givenness by adumbrations, which characterizes perception, does not lead from an immanent content to a transcendent object, but from a worldly aspect to an object that appears in it. Moreover, it is undoubtedly because Husserl cannot differentiate between a worldly moment ("objective" in Patočka's sense) and a strictly objective moment, one constitutive of the object, that he situates the moments of manifestation on the subjective side. If the world is exclusively defined as a world of objects, if we refuse to recognize a subjective dimension in it in the precise sense in which it carries the trace of our life and bears witness to existences for which it appears, then manifestation as such, not being the object, will be subjective only in the sense of what is immanent in consciousness. We see that the split between manifestation and object that gives rise to a subjectivation of the adumbration relies on the refusal to recognize a meaning of the subjective that is not exclusive from worldly transcendence and therefore does not impose inscription in the immanence of a consciousness—or rather, this split relies on a displacement of the meaning of the subjective: "While 'subjective' was taken first in the commonly accepted meaning, designating the phenomenal (and, in this sense, 'objective') that takes into consideration perspectives, modes of givenness, positional characteristics of modalization, our approach to things, different from things in themselves (that are without perspective), the subjective as experienced is distinguished from the phenomenal that appears in the experienced."[19]

However, it should be pointed out again that any substitution of the subjective as lived experience for the worldly subjective relies in the final analysis on a certain idea of the objective. The entire difficulty is to conceive of a sense of the "objective" that will not be reduced to that of the *blosse Sache* [mere thing], a dimension of the object in which my existence is reflected and which varies with the movements of my body, in short, a dimension in which the subjective in the sense of phenomenal can be inscribed.

After having postulated the split between the hyletic moment and the corresponding objective moment, we must, as it were, "restitch" what has been torn asunder and account for the manifestation of a world by starting from the subjective understood as subjectivity—in other words, from the immanence of consciousness. Now, this transcendental analysis, which is in reality a reconstruction, faces insurmountable difficulties. They center on the notion of noesis, a mysterious concept whose specific function is to allow the hyletic datum to rejoin the objectivity from which it was originally severed, accounting for the movement of adumbrating; this is a concept that bears the burden of intentionality. Insofar as the material of perception is constituted from immanent givens, the act that gives them meaning must be homogeneous with them; it must also be a lived experience. Moreover, how can a lived experience transcend the sphere of immanence to which it belongs by its essence so as to confer on sensible matter a figurative function? How can it give rise within the hyletic content to the spatial dimension that belongs to it as a moment of an object? How can a lived experience, as it were, by its own means transcend the sphere of immanence and account for the meaning of transcendence that is constitutive of the perceived reality? The difficulty stems from the fact that the lived experience is defined as what can legitimately be given in reflection, what can become the object of an internal perception. Indeed, it is unquestionable that the world is experienced in the sense that it appears to someone, that it is "subjective" according to the accepted meaning formulated earlier.

But the recognition of this fact in no way prejudices what we must understand exactly by lived experience and the sense of the being of the subjective. It could very well be that the subjective being of the world excludes precisely reference to a content accessible in reflection; that the lived being of the world does not contradict its transcendence; indeed, that the appearance of the subjective—the *cogito*—is originally dependent on the manifestation of the world. In any case, this is what we will attempt to show. However, this is in no way Husserl's perspective; the subjective being of the world refers to the composition of perception out of lived experiences, so that the intentionality that unfolds the distance of the object is first given to itself in an immanent manner. Now, how can what is given to itself produce a transcendence? How can what is its own manifestation make something else appear? If the noesis is a lived experience, it smothers itself such that there is no place in it for anything other than itself.[20] The givenness of the objective moment by the noesis is incomprehensible because the opening upon a transcendence by a lived experience is inconceivable.[21] Such is undoubtedly the reason, as Patočka points out following Tugendhat, that Husserl never inquires into how the noetic lived experience is given to itself; to confront this point of the weakness of the constitutive edifice might result in dangerously destabilizing it.

Thus Husserl can maintain the thesis that the givenness of the object is the animation of a sensible matter by a noesis only on the condition that he abandon his account of the effective transcendence of the world, which is to say of this dimension of the world that is precisely irreducible to a givenness of meaning. The subjectivation of appearance in the form of immanent lived experiences could only lead to a *subjectivation of the appearing*—in other words, to a transcendental idealism that, in regard to its ability to account for what interests us here, takes us no farther than Kant's transcendental idealism. Instead of showing how the subject is in the world (in the sense that it contributes to the manifestation of a transcending of which it forms a part), Husserl, as it were, puts the world in the subject. This is tantamount to saying that the passage to the level of lived experiences, to the level of contents, leads inevitably to a dismembering of appearance according to the duality of the hyletic and the noetic, a dismembering that appears to be irreversible; once we have split off manifestation as an autonomous content from the objective moment it adumbrates, we can never rejoin the figure of the phenomenon. Within this duality and this remarkable unity of matter and form that Husserl talks about, duality prevails over unity, which thus remains an abstract unity. Either one returns to the level of the subjective understood as lived experience (but then one is led to subject appearance to the law of the object, to divide it, which leaves one unable to understand how a lived experience can confer an ostensive function on a sensory content) or one recognizes the originary and therefore untearable character of appearance as givenness by adumbrations (in which case one must relinquish one's recourse to subjectivity such as Husserl understands it and think with new consequences about this lack of distinction between manifestation and appearing that was thematized earlier).

Therefore it seems indisputable that the way in which Husserl thematizes perceptual appearance misses its phenomenological distinctiveness. The goal of the *épochè* is to check this "capitation" by manifestation, which always leads to its reconstitution on the basis of the appearing being, in order to elucidate the very dimension of phenomenality, of appearance in its autonomy. The phenomenon is in fact presentation through and through; it is its own disappearing to the benefit of the appearing, which means that one must neither confuse it with the appearing (with a simple thing) nor separate it from the appearing, because this would again amount to making it into a kind of thing. It is to this, however, that Husserl ultimately resigns himself when he has recourse to a theory of lived experiences; he does not succeed in preserving the autonomy of the phenomenal, its necessary independence vis-à-vis any ontic figure. Instead of understanding the subjective as the phenomenal, or at the very least in terms of the latter, he approaches the phenomenal from the subjective conceived of as a certain category of contents. This is tantamount to saying that Husserl does not succeed in conceiving of appearance (the subjective) other than as self-givenness; according to him there is solid affirmation of an appearance only to the extent that this appearance itself can be given in an intuition, the object of an internal perception. The evidence of the subjective (of the appearance) bracketing of the appearing necessarily is immediately interpreted as immanent givenness—as grasping an internal content. The being of the subjective consists in this ability to be reflected in the identity of its being and appearance, whence the determination of the subjective as lived experience and the failure of a reconstitution of appearance. There is thus without question a Cartesianism in Husserl that is expressed especially in the difficulty he experiences in separating himself from certain Brentanian theses. However, this Cartesianism finds both its roots and its ultimate expression in the intuitionist and therefore objectivist determination of fulfillment. The satisfaction that responds to the need for fullness is immediately interpreted as the presence of the object, as the exclusion of any form of deficiency or distance. The thinglike characteristic sense of fullness prevails over its "affective" sense. In other words, the structural relation of emptiness and fulfillment, as will be shown shortly, has a considerable scope; it is interpreted as the *opposition* between deficient givenness and intuition. Thus there is evidence (satisfaction) and presence only as givenness of the thing as it is in itself: "The certitude of self from the existence of the *ego*, of the *sum*, is interpreted as presence, presence as originary self-givenness. Moreover, originary self-givenness requires a corresponding object. Whence, the supposition of the act of consciousness, of the noesis originarily understandable in reflection."[22]

Thus the recourse to lived experience as the ultimate basis and the intuitionist interpretation of fulfillment as the givenness of the object appear as two aspects of the same attitude. As Patočka again observes, "Intuition designates the mode of givenness of an object, while fulfillment can also take place where no object, no thing nor existing thing-like process can be emphasized."[23] It is particularly important to ask whether the fulfillment corresponding to the cogito—the test of my existence as certitude—can be interpreted as intuition as the self-givenness of lived experience. If it is true that the subjective initially signifies the appearance of the world, such that the "subject" of this appearance is essentially dependent on the revelation of a world, the certitude of my existence first has as its "content" that of the world and so no longer stands in contradiction with a certain absence to myself, thus with a certain "emptiness." If it turns out that I meet myself only beginning with the world, on a level with its "subjective" dimension, if my own appearance is inscribed in the anonymous appearance of the world so to speak, then there is a presence to self only as a distance from self, and I understand myself (fill myself) only as absent to myself.

Be that as it may, in supporting the appearance itself over an originary appearing (the lived experience) Husserl betrays the radicality of the phenomenological reduction. The fact that this appearing is not given by profiles but is instead characterized by the identity of its being and its manifestation does not change the fact that the autonomy of the phenomenal is entirely compromised. Appearance as appearance of things is completely dependent on a specific manifestation and therefore on the positing of an appearing being, the lived experience. In determining the appearance on the basis of the lived experience, Husserl abides by the phenomenological requirement that prescribes regressing from the appearing, whatever it might be, to its appearance; he remains therefore, in regard to the lived experience, on the level of the natural attitude. Indeed, as Patočka writes, "There is a phenomenal field, a being of the phenomenon as such, that cannot be reduced to any being which appears at its center and which it is therefore impossible to explain from being, *whether the latter be a naturally objective species or egologically subjective.*"[24]

In this context, there is a lack of unitarian concept of the phenomenal that would include the natural reality and the lived experience and that would thus allow one to bridge the eidetic abyss that Husserl regards as separating consciousness and reality. But such a concept assumes a more radical *époché*, one that permits devitalization of the positing of the lived experience as self-evident and therefore finished with the pseudoevidence of consciousness.

Nevertheless, it is undoubtedly in the perceived, and in the presuppositions that underlie its description, that we must look for the ultimate root of this subjectivation of phenomenality. As was noted at the outset, if perception is givenness "in the flesh" this in no way means that it fulfills the empty intentionality, that it confers on it an absolute fullness. The perception of something involves only signitive moments; it is characterized by the gap between the thing itself focused upon and its manifestations, which are necessarily partial and incomplete. In other words, the thing "just as it is in itself" is always absent; it exceeds by its nature the series of its manifestations. The entire difficulty is to correctly interpret this absence of the thing in its adumbrations, this inevitable gap between the appearing and its manifestations—the fact that the thing itself is never presented in what presents it. The distance inherent in the manifestation is interpreted by Husserl as the duality and the unity of the *hylé* and the noesis. The actual aspect is not the thing, but it is nevertheless its appearance to the extent that it is animated by a noesis that focuses upon it. The thing as such is really absent from its adumbration, but it is present intentionally as noema, insofar as an act apprehends it within the adumbration, thus conferring on the latter the function of appearance; the absence of the thing in the adumbration represents the other side of the coin, its presence in consciousness. If any perception is necessarily incomplete, in the sense that the thing in itself is always absent from what presents it, it is nevertheless always a perception *of the thing*, once this void is filled in advance by the noesis. Thus the excess of the thing vis-à-vis the adumbration that characterizes perception is at the same time (intentional) belonging of the thing to consciousness. Everything therefore happens as if the nonintuitive moments (strictly speaking, non-sensed) implied in perception—everything that, regarding the thing, is not given—could have only a subjective existence, as if the subjective were the index of the nonintuitive. Such is exactly the meaning of the assimilation established from the outset by Husserl between the signitive-intuitive pair on the one hand and the emptiness-fulfillment pair on the other; pure meaning is valid for the absent object (or rather refers to the thing as absent). Moreover, this determination of the nonintuitive as subjective existence itself presupposes that the nonintuitive is pure-and-simple absence, that emptiness is nongivenness rather than a specific mode of givenness. Such is without question the deepest root of the subjectivation of appearance in Husserl's world: the inability of conceiving of the absence or the deficiency as a constitutive moment of phenomenality, as an "objective" moment. Husserl spontaneously understands absence as the inverse of a presence rather than as constitutive of presence; put in another way, "emptiness" is what cannot be, what has no reality, which is why an absence from the objective point of view can only refer to a subjective reality. Moreover, "we can ask ourselves if emptiness is a 'simple intention' that fulfillment converts into the fulfilled in person, so that it disappears itself, or indeed if it also conceals something positive, a given."[25] Of course, the answer is contained in the question because "if we examine in depth the theory of modes of givenness, it will certainly become evident that the 'non-intuitive' that appears in a deficient mode of givenness is also a being, a being that is not of a subjective-egological nature."[26] Thus in the final analysis the subjectivation of appearance refers to the purely negative determination of emptiness as nongivenness—in other words, to the refusal to recognize as phenomenological given the dimension of absence that is constitutive of perception; the absence of the object to the adumbration necessarily conceals its presence to consciousness by virtue of intentionality. Inversely, a critique of subjectivism, of the composition of perception on the basis of lived experiences, involves recognition of the positivity of absence as a specific mode of the given and therefore a *reevaluation of the status of the structure emptiness-fulfillment*. A consistent phenomenology cannot ignore an inquiry into the sense of being of "nonbeing."

Such a negative notion of absence conceals an objectivist conception of presence. In effect, to deny emptiness the status of a mode of given is to postulate that a thing is not present if it does not present *itself* (so to speak, exhaustively) in its manifestations; it is to posit that there is fulfillment only as adequate possession of the object. Thus the denial of the phenomenological positivity of "emptiness" is merely an expression of the assimilation carried out by Husserl between the structural relation of empty intentionality and fulfillment on the one hand and the contrast between the deficient mode of givenness and the presence of the object on the other. To conceive of fulfillment as the presence of the thing itself is ipso facto to interpret all partiality or indetermination as a deficient mode of givenness. It is to understand the focus upon emptiness as a lacking; it is to deny any positivity to absence. Moreover, in describing perception as givenness by adumbrations, Husserl seems to recognize a certain distance, a certain lack of presence as constitutive of perception. To say that for God himself the transcendent would be given by adumbrations is to recognize that the absence of the thing "as it is in itself" is not a deficiency susceptible to being fulfilled but a constitutive characteristic of appearance. To affirm that the adumbration is not an appearance since it gives the thing in the flesh is to recognize that the partiality of givenness is its very condition. Husserl himself affirms that perception is naturally "inadequate": "Necessarily there always remains a horizon of determinable indeterminateness, no matter how far we go in our experience, no matter how extensive the continua of actual perceptions of the same thing may be through which we have passed. No god can alter that, no more than the circumstance that $1 + 2 = 3$, or that any other eidetic truth obtains."[27]

Thus the clarification that Husserl proposes regarding the composition of perception is based on presuppositions that contradict what a rigorous description of perception provides. Everything occurs as if there were two competing conceptions of the object. The first, which is supported by phenomenality itself, grasps the object directly through perception and recognizes in it a constitutive indeterminacy. The second conceives of the presence of the object only as adequate givenness and therefore interprets the indeterminacy of perception as a deficiency or a fault. This duality corresponds to two characterizations of intuition that continually mingle and merge imperceptibly into each other throughout the Husserlian corpus. The first grasps intuition as presence in the flesh, as proof that "it is the thing itself"; it is meeting with the thing in its being *there*, in contrast to the signitive intentionality, and it does not exclude a dimension of absence or distance. One could say that here fulfillment is a *satisfaction*. The other involves intuition as the presence of the thing in itself, as proof of an adequacy; it is a grasping of the thing according to the plenitude of its determinations, in contrast with empty intentionality, and it therefore excludes any lacuna, any indeterminacy. Fulfillment in this context is *filling up an emptiness*. Moreover, this last idea of intuition and object, which unquestionably dominates constitutive analysis, is already at work on the very level of the description of perception. The latter is in effect characterized by a fundamental ambiguity, by a tension between two radically different ontological attitudes, as if the description in its purity were always already concealed by a conceptuality that betrays it.

This is clearly visible in the *Logical Investigations* in which Husserl's difficulty is evident, particularly so in section 14 of the *Sixth Logical Investigation*, which aims precisely at characterizing perception:

Perception, so far as it claims to give us the object "itself," really claims thereby to be no mere intention, but an act, which may indeed be capable of offering fulfilment to other acts, but which itself requires no further fulfilment. But generally, and in all cases of "external" perception, this remains a mere pretension. The object is not actually given, it is not given wholly and entirely as that which it itself is.[28]

Husserl does not succeed in distinguishing clearly between perceptual presence ("in the flesh") and adequate givenness. In effect, in affirming that the givenness of the object "itself" involves the pretension of an ultimate fulfillment, Husserl assimilates simultaneously the givenness of the object itself and adequate givenness. This he clarifies immediately with regard to external perception that does not achieve this claim, by saying that the object in this context is not given "as it is in itself." However, if in perception the object is not given such as it is in itself, it obviously cannot be given itself either. To say that it is not given as it is in itself is tantamount to saying that it is given as it is not or other than that it is, which is ultimately to say that it is not given *itself.* From this point on, by characterizing perception in this way Husserl misses its specificity, since if the adumbration does not give the object as it is in itself then it gives it such as it is for the perceiving person, in which case it cannot be distinguished from a common appearance. The introduction of a determination of intuition as fulfillment that itself no longer needs any fulfillment (in other words, as adequate givenness) immediately compromises the possibility of characterizing perception as givenness in the flesh; if there exists an object "in itself" as a closed system of determinations susceptible to ultimate fulfillment, we can no longer define perception, which is always partial, as the givenness of the *thing itself*. In fact, Husserl immediately realizes the difficulty, since he adds several lines later:

We must, however, note that the object, as it is *in itself*—in the only sense relevant and understandable in our context, the sense which the fulfillment of the perceptual intention would carry out—is *not wholly different* from the object realized, however imperfectly, in the percept.[29]

However, what does it mean to say that the object in itself is not "totally other" than its perceived being? How can an alterity not be total? The examination of these texts concerning fulfillment largely confirms this analysis. What intention focuses upon improperly, fulfillment "*sets directly before us*, or at least more directly than the intention does. In fulfilment our experience is represented by the words: 'This is the thing *itself*.' This 'itself' must not be understood too strictly, as if there must be some percept bringing the object itself to actual phenomenal presence."[30]

Once again, the idea of perception as intuition is immediately threatened by the recourse to a determination of intuition as adequacy, in relation to which the difference between intention and perception becomes blunted. To say that perception gives the thing in a "more direct" way than does intention is tantamount to saying that it does not give it directly (there are no degrees of meaning to the word *direct*) and therefore to contradicting the idea of givenness in the flesh. Likewise, to affirm that the *itself* in "this is the thing itself" must not be understood in the strict sense is to recognize, as in fact Husserl explicitly does incidentally, that perception does not ultimately give the *thing itself* (there is no meaning of "this is the thing itself" other than the strict sense!). Here again, the intervention of another meaning of intuition, as absolute fullness, compromises the determination of perception as givenness in person. A reading of the continuation of the text just cited confirms that such is indeed the thrust of Husserl's hesitations:

The relativity of this 'directness,' this 'self,' points further to the fact that the relation of fulfillment is of a sort that admits of degrees. A concatenation of such relations seems accordingly possible where the epistemic superiority steadily increases. Each such ascending series points, however, to an *ideal limit*, or includes it as a final member, a limit setting an unsurpassable goal to all advances: *the goal of absolute knowledge, of the adequate self-presentation of the object of knowledge.*[31]

We see that the attempt to characterize perceptual fulfillment as "direct" givenness of the thing itself is immediately compromised by the introduction of a horizon of absolute adequacy. From the point of view of this acceptance of the meaning of intuition, givenness by adumbrations can no longer signify givenness of the thing itself, since it is never givenness of the thing as it is in itself, and the adumbration is then degraded inevitably in appearance. This approach to perception from the ideal of adequate knowledge compromises the possibility of grasping its specificity. Either one respects the essentially inadequate and indeterminate character of perception (in which case it no longer makes any sense to use the ideal of an adequate presentation of the object and to speak of the thing "as it is in itself") or one clings to this ideal of adequacy, without verifying its phenomenological validity (and one therefore defines a closed essence of the thing beyond the infinite course of its manifestations). But if one does so, it becomes impossible to reconcile the inadequate character of perception with its capacity for attaining the thing itself and thus for distinguishing an adumbration from an appearance. It becomes clear that, in the first case, the partiality of perception is constitutive of givenness, while in the second case it is its negation. Furthermore, it should be noted that introduction of this horizon of adequacy reduces the difference between empty intentionality and perceptual fulfillment—neither of which attains the thing as it is in itself— and thus conflicts with the thesis, advanced by Husserl himself, of an eidetic abyss between the signitive intentionality and intuition, whatever that may be.

One could certainly retort that these misgivings can be explained by the realist ontology that still underpins the *Logical Investigations* and that the transcendental clarification should remove all these ambiguities.[32] But it is not that simple because, despite the abandonment of the realist meaning of the thing in itself, the tension that characterizes the *Logical Investigations* can also be found in the description of the perceived in *Ideas I*. Although showing that perception is characterized by the appearing standing behind its manifestation, that the adumbration is therefore the unity of a presentation and a concealing (so that no adumbration can in principle reduce the distance that separates it from what it makes appear), Husserl continues to use the vocabulary of *imperfection* and *inadequacy*. In so doing, he engraves, so to speak, the horizon of an adequate givenness that the concept of adumbration is intended to contest. Granel makes this quite clear: "To say that the 'sensory data,' as adumbrations in which from the beginning and constantly 'the thing itself' is profiled, give me however *only* always fragmentary aspects of it . . . is, whatever our intention, to maintain the myth of an indefinite, progressive and indefinitely limited emergence of reality in appearance." It is therefore not seeing that "if we declare perception inadequate on 'principle,' it is therefore no longer *inadequate* at all, since the idea of adequacy has no meaning on its own, other than that of a misinterpretation, and is opposed to its principle."[33]

Nevertheless, it is true that Husserl thematizes this difficulty in Part Four of *Ideas*. It takes the form of a contradiction between the principle of "the absence of limits of objective reason" and the eidetic specificity of perceptual experience. This principle establishes the equivalence between a thesis of existence and a rational thesis, between being and full determinability. It is this principle that is expressed in the structure of empty intentionality and fulfillment inasmuch as it signifies an aspiration of the focus on fullness, on the adequate presentation of the object only focused upon. Thus Husserl writes: "*To every 'truly existing' object* there corresponds *the idea of a possible consciousness* in which the object itself is seized upon *originarily* and therefore in a *perfectly adequate* way. Conversely, if this possibility is guaranteed, then *ipso facto* the object truly exists."[34]

How can we reconcile this thesis with the discovery of the fact that objects exist—those that are attained in an external perception, that cannot by their nature be given in an adequate way, in other words according to an integral determination? How can we make sure that despite its eidetic characteristics the perceived object can respond to what is required by the existence of all objects? Clearly, the only solution consists in integrating in the definition of object in itself the constitutive lack of fulfillment of the perceived object and therefore in defining the object "itself" as the pole of unlimited progress of experience, which is to say as the unity of an infinity of determinations. Such an object obviously cannot be given since it is essentially that whose givenness is indefinitely differentiated. However, one has an idea of this object as the pole of an infinite flow because "the idea of an infinity motivated in conformity with its essence is not itself an infinity; seeing intellectually that this infinity of necessity cannot be given does not exclude, but rather requires, the intellectually seen givenness of the *idea* of this infinity."[35] One might as well say that the object, inasmuch as it envelops the infinite, cannot be given "as it is in itself" and that adequate givenness has a *regulating* rather than a constitutive meaning. This solution therefore allows reconciliation of two apparently contradictory requirements: adequate givenness of the object and the infinite flow of perceptual adumbrations. However, it is at the cost of a change in point of view; the thing itself, as it is profiled in perception, is now nothing but an idea and therefore has merely a subjective existence. This is what consciousness must posit so that the flow of adumbrations can be grasped as a process of infinite determination.

Yet, does the recourse to the idea "in the Kantian sense" represent a true solution? Does it not appear instead to be a compromise solution that points out the problem rather than really solving it? This is because in truth an adequate givenness of the thing remains incompatible with the eidetic of the perceived, and the Husserlian solution consists only in distributing each of the requirements on distinct levels, which is tantamount to recognizing that they are incompatible. Since perception reveals an absolutely original mode of givenness, which radically calls into question the rationalist requirement of exhaustive givenness, Husserl can maintain this requirement only by denying it a constitutive character precisely by recognizing in it the status of simple requirement: to speak of an idea in the Kantian sense is to name what is required while remaining all the while unrealizable. It therefore confirms, without wanting to recognize it, the defeat of a certain idea of the object, and therefore of reason, in the face of the evidence of experience. The Kantian idea resolves nothing; it integrates the nostalgia of the rational in the interpretation of perception. Part Four of *Ideas I* therefore appears to reveal only the tension that is present beginning with the *Logical Investigations*, a tension between the discovery of the singular figure of the perceived and the implementation of thinking, stemming from a rationalist conception of being manifestly incapable of achieving the specificity of perception. This thinking defines being as what is legitimately fully determinable, in other words as object; perception, as givenness by adumbrations, is characterized by the constitutive indetermination of the appearing; the nonpresentation of what appears in the manifestation is not the reverse of an adequate presentation, which would be theoretically possible, but the very condition of the manifestation. For Husserl, in keeping with the tradition he follows, it is evident that experience is fundamentally knowledge, that consequently being is what is legitimately fully determinable and therefore that there is a relation to what is only based on the mode of intuition, understood as saturated vision or fulfilled need. The subjectivism that characterizes Husserl's phenomenology is the inevitable consequence of this presupposition, which can be qualified as *objectivist*.

The principle of the absence of limits of objective reason and therefore the characterization of what appears as susceptible to becoming the object of adequate givenness has as a consequence a subjectivation of appearing that is, as it were, redoubled. To posit the appearing as object is inevitably to compromise the specificity of the adumbration—which gives the thing itself only as indeterminable as its own absence—and it is therefore to push the adumbration toward appearance, toward the subjective. If the object is assembled beyond the adumbration, as a pole of integral determinability, the adumbration is thereby separated from the object; unable to give the object itself, the manifestation deteriorates in appearance. On the other hand, one must still account for the function of manifestation, and it is on this level that objectivism gives rise to a redoubling of the subjectivation that at first took the form of an assimilation of the adumbration into an immanent given. From an objectivist perspective, to say that the object is *only* adumbrated in the manifestation is to affirm that the object is really absent from the adumbration; according to Husserl the nonpresence of the object in the adumbration cannot be conceived of as a mode of the given. Moreover, to the degree that one must account for the figurative function of the adumbration, one must give oneself the object whose manifestation it is; its objective absence can therefore refer only to its subjective presence in the form of noematic pole. The function of manifestation is not compromised because the absence of the object in the adumbration signifies its presence to constituting consciousness. Thus the subjectivation of the manifestation in the form of *hylé* leads inevitably to a subjectivation of the appearing in the form of the noema, and the inability of the event to be torn from the manifestation is conceived of as a real composition of lived experiences the diversity of which no mode of relation, including an *hylé*-morphic one, will succeed in overcoming its diversity. In this sense, one can say that Husserl does not succeed in moving beyond the alternative between empiricism and intellectualism; he is satisfied with juxtaposing them. It can be seen that displacement of the meaning of phenomenality—autonomization of the subjective—is the consequence and the counterpart of autonomization of the objective. It is because the appearing is posited as an object beyond its appearance that the manifestation is separated from what appears in it and is thus situated near a subject. The event of the appearance is missed by default in positing an object transcending its own manifestations and, as a result, by excess in positing a subject in which the manifestations of thing flow back in the form of pure lived experiences. The apparent opposition between objectivism and subjectivism conceals a profound complicity: object and subject are the two residua of a same split in appearance. In other words, if appearance is conceived of as *presentation* of the object *itself* in its manifestations, the being of appearance can consist only in a *re-presentation* and must therefore be defined as *consciousness*.

It is these presuppositions and their consequences, which have been given the form of what is called "transcendental phenomenology," that Husserl's description of perception shakes to its very foundations. The result is a quandary, one that is constitutive of emerging phenomenology and that can easily be shown to recur in all areas of Husserl's thought. The only way to extricate oneself from this quandary is to cling to experience, to think in accordance with perception rather than against it, to try to gauge the philosophical changes it prescribes; it is a question of reforming one's mode of thinking with respect to appearance. Such a requirement is eminently phenomenological since it consists in rigorously adhering to the "things themselves," to what is given according to the limits in which it is given, in bringing experience—still silent—to the pure expression of its own meaning, to use Husserl's phrase that Merleau-Ponty was fond of quoting. This requirement of returning to appearance as such and of redefining our categories in connection with it outlines the program of a phenomenological reduction.

Phenomenological Reduction as Critique of Nothingness

Phenomenological reduction (understood in the broad sense, which encompasses the moment of *épaché* and that of reduction strictly speaking) is defined by Husserl as suspension the natural attitude. This strategy is characterized by the thesis that the world's existence is a unique spatiotemporal reality subsisting in self that has for its purpose the elucidation of the proper phenomenality of the world that has been neutralized. It does not consist in a negation of the world's existence with a view toward the discovery of a being whose existence would be certain beyond doubt; it suspends the thesis of existence so as to allow an inquiry into its sense of being. The *épaché* is diverted from the naïve positing of the appearing in order to question the very structure of its appearance. It is therefore the attempt of thinking without presuppositions, which requires that one account for appearance itself without borrowing from the structures of the appearing that appears in and through it.[1] Moreover, we have attempted to show that in effective implementation of the reduction Husserl remains dependent on unquestioned presuppositions that compromise the radical nature of his undertaking. More precisely, he conceives of appearance as relying on a specific appearing, the lived experience, whose own appearance is not truly questioned precisely because in the final analysis, the structure of the appearance itself is not clearly distinguished from the structure of the appearing, which we spontaneously tend to grasp as object. The definition of the appearance's structure is dependent on the rationalist *telos* of adequate givenness, of an ideal that is valid only on the level of the appearing and cannot therefore command the determination of the appearance. It follows from this that an authentic phenomenological reduction faithful to the task Husserl set forth must give itself the means of truly liberating appearance from its subjection to the very characteristics of the appearing, neutralizing this kind of objectivist presupposition that undermines Husserl's work. It must grasp therefore the natural attitude on a more profound level than Husserl did; it must elucidate the secret thesis, the "thesis of existence," in an entirely distinctive sense, one that, as will become clear, dictates the undue subjection of appearance to the object.

Such is in a way the task to which Merleau-Ponty dedicates himself in the last chapter of *The Visible and the Invisible*. In it he attempts to clarify his own position vis-à-vis phenomenology and therefore to identify what constitutes, in his view, the essential limitation of Husserl's phenomenology. He situates it in the original determination of phenomenology as *eidetic*, or rather, in a certain conception of essence that compromises the implementation of the watchword of faithfulness to phenomena. In effect, the *épaché* questions the meaning of being of what is without doubt and characterizes it as meaning. Yet, instead of regrasping the meaning of this meaning in the light of phenomenality in which it is demonstrated, phenomenology determines it in advance as a positive being, as an *essence*. In other words, far from redefining the meaning—which is nothing but the being—for us of what is, the appearance itself—as based on its own structure, which has been separated out by the *épaché*—phenomenology subordinates the description of appearance to a preliminary conception of the meaning that apprehends it as a positive being. In a kind of inversion that constitutes the very naïveté of Husserl's phenomenology, experience is reconstituted on the basis of essences; it is transferred wholly to the level of essence, while in reality essence always proceeds from experience and never absorbs it completely. As Merleau-Ponty writes:

The essence is certainly dependent. The inventory of the essential necessities is always made under a supposition (the same as that which recurs so often in Kant): if this world is to exist for us, or if there is to be a world, or if there is to be something, then it is necessary that they observe such and such a structural law. But whence do we get the hypothesis, whence do we know that there is something, that there is a world? This knowing is beneath the essence, it is the experience of which the essence is a part and which it does not envelop.[2]

Thus to determine being as essence is to ignore the thesis of world that essence always presupposes and whose sense of being must be questioned for itself. Far from the "thesis of world" (appearance itself) possibly being absorbed in the transparent manifestation of essence, the latter actually refers—as all manifestations do—to the very structure of appearance, to the emergence of a "there is" that remains the privileged object of description. Merleau-Ponty shows clearly the thrust of what we called the objectivism of Husserlian phenomenology, the subjection of phenomenality to the appearing conceived of as pure object, endowed with intrinsic determinations that can be legitimately grasped adequately as essence. Indeed, phenomenology reveals the naiveté of the natural attitude that conceives of existence as the subsistence in self of an existent; it uncovers the constitutive dimension of appearance, in subordinating this appearance to a self-sufficient being—that has as its only privilege to appear as it is, to realize the identity of being and thought—it demonstrates the same naiveté that it initially criticized. Merleau-Ponty then demonstrates rigorously the difficulties with which the Husserlian concept of essence inevitably finds itself confronted. They can be summarized in the contradiction between the necessity of a mediation (the eidetic variation that is supported on the basis of worldly experience) and the possibility of an intuition of essence. The grasp of essence proceeds from an arbitrary variation that aims at drawing out that whose suppression leads to the disappearance of the object as such:

It is from this test that the essence emerges—it is therefore not a positive being. It is an in-variant, it is exactly that whose change or absence would alter or destroy the thing; and the solidity, the essentiality of the essence is exactly measured by the power we have to vary the thing. A pure essence which would not be at all contaminated and confused with the facts could result only from an attempt at total variation.[3]

Either essence supposes the test of a variation that separates its constituting structures from experience (in which case variation could never arrive at a pure essence, owing to its inability to take sufficient distance from experience, to surmount the fact that it belongs to a world) or it is effectively accessible in transparence as a positive being (in which case variation would not be necessary since it would be justified only by the empirical inscription of the person who attempts to conceive of phenomena). Thus it is questionable whether it is still meaningful to speak of essence; since the subject who apprehends it, who is capable of a "total variation," has broken all connections with the world, what is missing is *that of which* essence is precisely the essence, namely the experience on which the variation is based. A pure essence would vanish in insignificance, to the extent that it lacked an existence of which it is the determination; ultimately it proves to be a contradictory concept.

Nevertheless, the goal of the present analysis is not to criticize Husserl's concept of essence but its *positivity*; the goal is to warn against the temptation to hypostatize essence, to conceive of it as positively or intuitively accessible, which is equivalent to separating it from that of which it is the essence. Intuitionism appears in this context as the opposite side of objectivism, in accordance with what was shown earlier. The whole difficulty lies in Husserl's claim to conceive of an eidetic intuition capable of "perceiving" (in a broader sense) essence, to grasp it directly as an "object," even though this essence is always based on or obtained at the conclusion of a variation. Husserl is correct in saying that variation does not produce essence but rather consciousness of essence insofar as it differs from an induction; yet, can consciousness of the essence be different from the individual's consciousness and stem from a specific intuition? Is not the nature of essence, on the contrary, to remain veiled within that of which it is the essence, to structure experience only as a "secret frame," a "principle of equivalence" that is nothing other than what it unifies, so that it cannot on principle become the object of a specific intuition? Such is, in any case, the perspective from which Merleau-Ponty develops his critique. It consists in revealing a sort of paradox at the heart of appearance since the appearing never appears *itself* in *its* manifestations; the invisible, which is the other name for essence, is the very condition of visibility.

Be that as it may, this critique is important for the purposes of the present study first in that it leads to what constitutes the ultimate source of objectivism. Indeed, shortly after the passage just quoted, Merleau-Ponty writes regarding variation:

In order to really reduce an experience to its essence, we should have to achieve a distance from it that would put it entirely under our gaze, with all the implications of sensoriality or thought that come into play in it, bring it and bring ourselves wholly to the transparency of the imaginary, think it without the support of any ground, in short, withdraw to the bottom of nothingness.[4]

The grasp of essence signifies a total variation, which itself supposes the denial of any belonging and refers to a "point of view" that is the point of view of nothingness itself. Thus, by demonstrating the last condition of a pure intuition of essence, Merleau-Ponty enables one to grasp the ultimate presupposition of objectivism: it consists in *the determination of the being's sense of being based on the prejudicial positing of nothingness.* This is confirmed in a text, published as an appendix by Lefort, in which Merleau-Ponty attempts to define the object according to its true appearance in contrast with how the natural attitude spontaneously conceives of it:

Starting with things taken in their native sense as identifiable nuclei, but without any power of their own, we arrive at the thing-object, at the In Itself, at the thing identical with itself, only by imposing upon experience an abstract dilemma which experience ignores. . . . The thing thus defined is not the thing of our experience, it is the image we obtain of it by projecting it into a universe where experience would not settle on anything, where the spectator would abandon the spectacle—in short, *by confronting it with the possibility of nothingness.*[5]

In other words, it is because objective thought approaches being on the basis of nothingness and determines it by confronting it with the possibility of nonbeing that being is defined as a pure object. Thus the objectivism that we believed we observed in Husserlian phenomenology would be subject to Bergson's critique of metaphysics, as it is laid out especially in *Creative Evolution.* This critique consists in showing that the history of metaphysics is structured around *false problems* that are themselves the consequence of an inversion of the orders of dependence within the real, the consequence of a cutting out of reality that does not respect its effective articulations.[6] These false problems are crystallized in the usage of the principle of sufficient reason, which consists in asking why something exists *rather than nothing.* This question is the prime example of the false question because it has as presupposition that nothingness can precede something, that being can emerge on the basis of nothing, which is tantamount (as becomes clear later) to reversing purely and simply the respective ontological status of being and nothingness. Now, if one takes seriously the various clues given by Merleau-Ponty and therefore the direction that his critique of the object seems to take, one must conclude that Husserlian phenomenology does not avoid metaphysics in the sense in which Bergson understands it. The natural attitude would not consist so much in a naiveté vis-à-vis the sense of the being of the world as in a blindness *concerning the sense of being of nothingness itself.* It would be this last presupposition that explains the primacy of a certain sense of the object at the center of the description of appearance and therefore commands the nonfulfillment of phenomenology. As a result, a consistent phenomenological reduction that seeks to confront what remains unthought in the sense of not thought in the thematization of phenomenality would not bear so much on the thesis of existence as on *the thesis of a preliminary nothingness,* by virtue of the last reason of objectivism. In this sense, phenomenological reduction would converge with Bergson's critique of metaphysics, and the return to the phenomenality of phenomena would not be foreign to Bergsonian intuition, understood as method, in the sense that Deleuze has brought to light. The phenomenological requirement would pass through an inquiry regarding the sense of being of nothingness, preliminary to the investigation of the sense of being of what is. Henceforth, reduction would lead one not from the suspension of this natural thesis to transcendental subjectivity but from the negation of a preliminary nothingness to the proper figure of appearance.

The examination of nothingness that opens chapter 4 of *Creative Evolution* responds to the need to approach "theoretical illusions" head on— the false problems that are posed for thought and that appeared to be obstacles to Bergson's investigations concerning life and evolution. It involves more precisely, by questioning nothingness, accounting for the ontological devalorization that evolution has been the subject of since the dawn of metaphysical thinking. One could therefore say that the critique of the principle of sufficient reason is dictated by the necessity to ontologically rehabilitate duration. The fundamental theoretical illusion, the one inherent in the spontaneous exercise of reflection to the point of constituting "the hidden spring, the invisible mover of philosophical thinking,"[7] consists in asking why something exists *rather than nothing*. This question itself includes a certain idea of existence as what emerges from the depths of nothingness, as a victory over nothingness: "I say to myself that there might be, that indeed there ought to be, nothing, and I then wonder that there is something. Or I represent all reality extended on nothing as on a carpet: at first was nothing, and being has come by super-addition to it."[8] Being is something that comes to be added to nothingness because there is less in the representation of nothingness than in the representation of something. It follows that what exists is necessarily characterized as fully determined, as a logical rather than a physical or psychological reality. From the moment that being is what is placed in balance with nothingness, it can only be to the degree that it possesses the wherewithal to resist nothingness, to the degree that it *is* as fully as the nothingness that threatens it *is not*. It is therefore absolutely determined because the smallest indetermination would mean its absorption by nonbeing, for it would not be at all if it were not fully; being is through and through *what it is*, a pure presentation of itself. Being can be only what escapes the question of the reason of its existence, only what is of such a nature that it did not start to exist; it can be only what draws its necessity from itself. Such is in fact the nature of logical existence, "that it seems to be self-sufficient and to posit itself by the effect alone of the force immanent in truth."[9] Briefly stated: "If we pass (consciously or unconsciously) through the idea of the nought in order to reach that of Being, the Being to which we come is a logical or mathematical essence, therefore non-temporal. And, consequently, a static conception of the real is forced on us: everything appears given once for all, in eternity."[10]

Such is, in Bergson's view, the ontological discredit to which duration is subjected within the metaphysical tradition. An existence that endures, that becomes and therefore does not possess the characteristic immutability of logical being, is not sufficiently strong to vanquish nothingness and posit itself; it is equivalent to a nonbeing. It follows that the ontological rehabilitation of duration is achieved by an "immediate" approach to being, without any interposition of nothingness. Moreover, if it is true that the passage through the idea of nothingness leads to a determination of being as logical being, one may legitimately conclude that a philosophy for which preeminent being is that which is entirely conceivable, susceptible to an adequate intuition, inevitably cuts being out from a background of nothingness. In other words, this philosophy approaches it from the point of view of the implicit question regarding its sufficient reason, which can then consist only in a fullness of determination. Such is undoubtedly the meaning of this note of *The Visible and the Invisible*, rarely quoted, that entrenches objectivism in an inevitable blindness of consciousness: "It disregards Being and prefers the object to it, that is, a Being with which it has broken, and which it posits beyond this negation, by negating this negation."[11] The "nonmediated" presence, the "nondissimulation of being," in the terms Merleau-Ponty uses in what follows, are posited as object because they are understood as the negation of a preliminary nothingness, as if it were necessary to break off our belonging to the world in order to reconstitute it abstractly. This is especially confirmed by an unpublished note from January 1960 in which Merleau-Ponty begins to elaborate the notion of what he calls *eminent* being:

It always assumes essentialist thinking—according to which there is something that in the last resort makes Being emerge—a necessary foundation, i.e., essential for the *there is*, a *nail* that anchors and establishes Being as absolutely opposed to Nothingness. Behind *eminent Being* there is a negative ontological base, as we say negative theology: definition of Being as what has surmounted, negated nothingness. This "not nothing" gives eminent Being only if we conceive of it starting with nothing. We must conceive of being from *not nothing*: non-hidden Being.

Such is unquestionably the implicit thought that commands the objectivism rife with meaning in a whole area of Husserlian phenomenology. One could say that the determination of being as nonhidden or nondissimulated that is imposed on the level of the strict description of perception is in competition—when it comes to interpreting this description—with a characterization of being as the negation of nothingness (in other words, ultimately as object). Everything happens as if nondissimulation, which is typical of something perceived that appears only in retreating behind what it presents, were itself only a sketch of an active negation of nothingness or indeterminacy, of an adequate givenness of the object "as it is in itself." One could therefore interpret the teleological structure of empty intentionality and fulfillment, the fact that emptiness "needs" fullness, as a sort of active expression of the metaphysical precedence of nothingness over being, as its subjective translation. The intention tends toward adequate fulfillment because nothingness can be abolished only by a fully determined reality, so that the perceived being, in which fulfillment always accompanies emptiness, cannot manifestly find a place in such a metaphysical economy. Moreover, what is valid for Husserl is a fortiori valid for Sartre; the Bergsonian critique of nothingness undoubtedly makes possible the establishment, in a critical way, of the unity of the two phenomenologies. The dialectic of the in-itself and the for-itself as the dialectic of being and nothingness, to which Merleau-Ponty devotes numerous pages in *The Visible and the Invisible*, can certainly be understood as the setting, refined and dramatized, of the metaphysical prejudice that consists in bringing being out against a background of nothingness that it must fill.

The critique of the principle of sufficient reason presupposes for its part a critique of the idea of nothingness and the genesis of this illusion. The principle of this critique, which is well known, consists in showing that there is more in nothingness than in being and not less, that nothingness therefore presupposes a preceding positing of being. Suffice it here to ask what is implied by the idea of abolition that is expressed in this manner: where there was something, now "there is no longer anything." When this is considered carefully, it becomes clear that this nothingness can in no way proceed from an experience. Even if I imagine the suppression of everything, I present myself necessarily as the one who accomplishes this suppression or for whom there is nothing; and I can disappear only if I present immediately another self for whom the former sinks into nothingness. Moreover, there is no absolute void in nature; the disappearance of an object necessarily signifies its replacement by another object, and if the latter is nothing the disappearance of the former leaves a determined void, which we call a place; it is still something. The idea of nothingness can in no way be based on an experience, whatever it may be, because there is always something, the flux of things, because fullness always follows upon fullness: "For a mind which should follow purely and simply the thread of experience, there would be no void, no nought, even relative or partial, no possible negation. Such a mind would see facts succeed facts, states succeed states, things succeed things."[12] Despite the appearance of banality, this assertion is of great significance. It indicates that all experiences are experiences of something; the essence of experience[13] implies the meeting with something real, however simple or indeterminate it may be, so that an experience that could refer to something other than what there is (to nonbeing) would not be an experience (it would unquestionably be something like a thought). Thus the experience of something peculiar *is always at the same time "experience" of the weight of being, of the encompassing by the world.*

From this comes the necessity of creating an idea of nothingness. It is converted into two positive elements: "*the idea, distinct or confused, of a substitution, and the feeling, experienced or imagined, of a desire or a regret.*"[14] The substitution of an object by another does not imply by itself any nothingness; the object that replaces the preceding one quite simply is. This substitution gives rise to negativity only on the condition that the mind remember the preceding state and prefer it to the actual situation: the latter will then be judged as being nothing in the sense that it is nothing of what was expected or hoped for. Thus we must add a valorization of the past to the memory of what was replaced, an enduring memory in current experience. In this regard, there is more and not less in the idea of an object as "not existing" than in the idea of this same object conceived of as existing; the consideration of the fact that this object replaces another and the psychological devalorization of the one that replaces are added to it.[15] It follows that the idea of an absolute nothingness, an abolition of everything— an idea presupposed by implementation of the principle of sufficient reason —is a contradictory idea, for abolition is possible only as substitution, and thus an idea of nothingness is possible only as circumscribed. As Bergson points out, if we analyze the idea of absolute nothingness, "we find that it is, at bottom, the idea of Everything, together with a movement of the mind that keeps jumping from one thing to another, refuses to stand still, and concentrates all its attention on this refusal by never determining its actual position except by relation to that which it has just left."[16]

Nothingness is in reality a *mirage*, in a tripartite sense that it assumes the horizon of perception, represents a reverse image of the real, and is the expression of a desire at the heart of a reality that does not lend itself to it. It vanishes therefore when consciousness seeks to approach and thematize it.[17] The determination of the real starting from nothingness proceeds in the final analysis from a confusion between the pragmatic order and the metaphysical order, from a projection onto reality such as it is in itself of the categories of the action that is the essential dimension of human existence: "It is unquestionable . . . that every human action has its starting-point in a dissatisfaction, and thereby in a feeling of absence. We should not act if we did not set before ourselves an end, and we seek a thing only because we feel the lack of it. Our action proceeds thus from 'nothing' to 'something,' and its very essence is to embroider 'something' on the canvas of 'nothing.'"[18]

The error of metaphysics consists therefore in extending the categories of action beyond their range of validity, in acting as if what norms the anthropological order were the very law of being. This is why the Bergsonian "reduction" always requires making a distinction between the two levels in order to attempt to restitute reality such as it is "in itself," independently of the categories of action. We find the complete formulation of this undertaking at the beginning of the last chapter of *Matter and Memory*, consisting of "the search for experience at its source, or rather above that decisive *turn* where, taking a bias in the direction of our utility, it becomes properly *human* experience."[19] Intuition, the Bergsonian representation of reduction, is something completely different from a return to the immediate, from a coincidence with what is presented; it demands a mediation and—as a torsion of the mind, crossing the categories of action—suspends the everyday world, ordered by utility, in order to rejoin a pre-human order.

In this regard, the reduction outlined by Merleau-Ponty is both close to and far from Bergsonian intuition. As for Bergson, it is a question of returning to a level that lies below that of idealization, of deformation, which itself is rooted in an action; it involves elucidating a territory yet unspoiled by any production. It is for this reason that Merleau-Ponty writes that philosophy must be "total reactivation, thinking from sedimentation, contact with total Being *before the separation of pre-theoretical life and of human*

Gebilde."[20] However, in contrast to Bergson, the production or creation established on the pretheoretical grounds of perception that form the layers of sediment is not restricted to the practical field; *it covers any extension of the production of meaning,* and if it is human it is such in a sense of a humanity that is implicated essentially in the structure of manifestation. Henceforth, we cannot, in principle, circumscribe a field of being short of the decisive turn and separate the order of intuition from that of action, because the turn has always already been made, because experience is originarily production, so that the prehuman or the pretheoretical is not something with which one can coincide. It is rather the depth of the unpresentable required by any presence. Whereas Bergson can situate experience short of the decisive turn because the latter has a circumscribed meaning—even if it essentially defines our humanity—Merleau-Ponty conceives of experience as *the decisive turn itself,* as creation on a foundation that is in principle invisible. In this sense Bergson is more Kantian than Merleau-Ponty despite all the distance he puts between himself and Kantianism.

Before drawing from the Bergsonian analysis the essential consequences regarding the meaning of phenomenological reduction, it is necessary to return briefly to the question of nothingness. Bergson's analysis can be summed up as a systematic critique of negativity, as a refusal of any positivation of the negative. The idea of a positive nothingness, even if circumscribed, is incompatible with the very meaning of experience. Bergson remarks that the negativity of the idea of nothingness is resolved by the addition of "two positive elements": the idea of substitution and the feeling of desire or regret. However, in the case of the second component, is a true positivity at issue? In more general terms, does not the very idea of the negative necessarily take root, so to speak, in an effective negativity?

The feeling that intervenes in the "false" idea of nothingness implies for its part several aspects. First, it includes a temporal component in which one would be wrong to see negativity because the presence of a memory in the present does not imply, in Bergson's view, any negation whatsoever; at issue here is a process of continuous growth that is maintained only by developing in heterogeneity, by creating qualitative differences. It involves a single mass that appears continually under different aspects, but with which it is entirely copresent. The past is therefore rigorously contemporary with the present to the point that the present is, strictly speaking, only the past at a higher degree of tension or of contraction.[21] Second, the intervention of desire or regret (which is merely a form of desire insofar as regretting is desiring that this something continue) inevitably introduces a "positively" negative dimension. There is no desire without the "feeling of absence," as Bergson himself recognizes; to desire is to focus on a reality as absent, and it is therefore to refer to nonbeing as such. Thus it does not suffice that consciousness remain fixed on what was replaced in order to live the new reality as nothingness; it is necessary that a disappointment be added, a disappointment that itself assumes that the past was desired. Moreover, to say that the past is desired is to recognize that it is focused upon as incomplete, and that at the very moment that it was still present *it was already experienced as incomplete.* In other words, it is not because one thing is replaced by another that I am going to regret it, desire it, focus upon it, and live the one that replaced it as negligible; all that can happen is that the loss reveals a desire that was not conscious when it was in the presence of its object. Rather, it is because I want the object still to be there that I am going to regret it and to experience the one that replaces it as equivalent to nothing.

Now, to say that I wanted the thing to last is to recognize that while the thing was still present *it was already experienced as lacking,* as not fulfilling the expectation that it created, as short of itself, of what it "promised." Thus the substitution realizes *a loss that was already constitutive of the relation to the present object.* So the Bergsonian construction is valid only on the condition that one admit a relation to presence in which a dimension of negativity intervenes since in desire the thing is grasped as its own absence. Bergson is therefore forced to reintroduce an authentically negative component that contradicts the affirmation according to which a mind in the presence of experience would remain ignorant of the idea of negation. Desire, assumed by the genesis of the idea of nothingness, is the test of a real nothingness in things.

It is true that Bergson can deny any reality to nothingness, citing the fact that feeling as such is positive. However, it is in this instance that he undoubtedly demonstrates a certain naïveté, at least from a phenomenological point of view. The fact that feeling as such is positive and bears on an object effectively present does not prevent this feeling from having, as possessor of meaning, the actual experience of a lack or an absence at the very center of presence; its material being cannot be confused with its intent. It is therefore, paradoxically by submission to a "positivist" conception of nothingness as pure nothingness, a conception that is the very one that he criticizes and that conceals a naïve idea of being, that Bergson remains blind to the authentic negativity implicit in the feeling of desire.

Everything happens as if nothingness could exist only as totally opposed to being. The critique of the principle of sufficient reason is carried out at the cost of a complete rejection of any negativity, as if it were still necessary to contain the threat of nothingness which Bergson demonstrates as stemming from a theoretical illusion.

Moreover, as becomes clear later, the fact that it is patently aberrant to posit an absolute nothingness against the background of which being would be cut out does not exclude but on the contrary allows introduction of a form of negativity into the everything of what is—in other words, into the world. If desire can indeed be reduced immediately to the confrontation between a positive feeling and a full reality, then taking into consideration desire's meaning reveals precisely a mode of negativity within things that does not provide an alternative to their presence.

The insufficient radicality of the Husserlian reduction (which consists precisely in its being a *reduction* to the region of consciousness) is due to Husserl's remaining dependent throughout his philosophical undertaking on the rationalist ideal of an adequate givenness and consequently on a spontaneous determination of being as object, a determination that enters into contradiction with the very structure of perception. The Husserlian *époché*, understood as elucidation of appearance itself, can therefore be brought to completion only if one suspends this objective presupposition, if one criticizes the structure of appearance without borrowing from the appearing that emerges in it. Moreover, demonstrating that the positing of a preliminary nothingness is the ultimate root of essentialist thinking and proceeding to a radical critique of the idea of nothingness as the absence of being, Bergson offers one the means of dealing successfully with this *époché*. The natural attitude is situated on a deeper level than Husserl himself understood it to be; it consists not in the thesis of a "unique spatio-temporal reality" so much as in the implicit positing of a positive nothingness that leads one inevitably to conceive of this unique reality as an ensemble of objects. Therefore the *époché*, whose function is to clarify the status of the thesis of existence characteristic of the natural attitude, to elucidate the true meaning of the being of this unique reality, can consist only in a suspension of this naïve idea, which is to say, the positive thesis of nothingness. Otherwise stated, what makes the thesis of existence problematic is not the thesis of the *existence* of a world so much as the determination of this world as an object. The naïveté does not reside in one thinking that there is a world there, but rather in admitting that it is governed by a principle of absolute determinability and that it can therefore be attained as it is *in itself.* It is in the objectivist characterization of the world that the naïve opposition between the in-itself and for-itself, between being and appearance, is rooted. Furthermore, the purpose of the *époché* is to rejoin the thesis of the world in its purity, precisely as thesis *of existence*; it is meant to grasp spontaneously the event of appearance before it is concealed by the appearing, to capture the pure burst of the "there is." This is why it must suspend what gives rise to the degradation of this "there is" in in-self (or in object), namely the thesis of a positive nothingness; it does not consist in suspension of the thesis of existence but in suspension of what compromises the access to the meaning of this thesis of existence. This explains why Husserl characterizes the *époché* in a negative way, even if this negation takes the form of a simple neutralization: would not this characterization refer precisely to the preliminary and implicit determination of being as an object? Husserl's purpose is certainly to clarify the sense of being of the world, but the fact that he proceeds by neutralizing the thesis of existence itself denounces a precomprehension of the world as object and, consequently, of existence as emergence from the depths of nothingness.

One could therefore advance the thesis that the Husserlian *époché*, as the means of accessing the sense of being of what exists, is the ultimate repetition (albeit one extremely refined) of the metaphysical dependence of being vis-à-vis nothingness; the suspension of the existence and the determination of what exists as an object, which results in reducing it to its constituted being, are aspects of the same act. The form that the reduction takes in *Ideas I* is in this regard extremely significant. After initially characterizing the *époché*, Husserl proceeds to analyze the physical thing and consciousness with the aim of showing the eidetic abyss that separates them; in contrast to the immanent perception that guarantees the existence of its object, the existence of the physical thing, the pole toward which the adumbrations converge, is never required as necessary by its own givenness. Thus Husserl summarizes: "Over against the positing of the world, which is a 'contingent' positing, there stands then the positing of my pure Ego and Ego-life which is a 'necessary,' absolutely indubitable positing. Anything physical which is given 'in person' can be non-existent: no mental process which is given 'in person' can be non-existent."[22]

This distinction makes possible the hypothesis of an annihilation of the world by nonagreement of the adumbration and leads to the disclosure of the absolute being of consciousness. It becomes clear in this context how the determination of the appearing as an object, as the infinite pole of the adumbrations, has as its opposite the possibility of the nonexistence of the world; the positing thesis of nothingness on which rests the "contingency" of the thesis of existence and the characterization of what exists as a pure object are metaphysical decisions that mutually govern each other. One could say that givenness by adumbrations is like the arrested image of the very emergence of being *against the backdrop of nothingness*, the threat to being by nothingness. Adumbrations are located in an extremely rigorous way between being and nothingness. Granel's commentary regarding the passage quoted earlier is significant (especially so since it is given from a perspective different from the one presented here):

Since matter is posited outside form, it is evident then that this convergence is purely contingent, since it is not grasped as the very essence of the "content," as its own "possibility." For Husserl, the object is *one* of the possibilities of the content; there is another: it is nothingness. Thus, Husserl finds himself caught up exactly in the very moment in which Leibniz fears not finding a response to the question: why is there being rather than nothing?[23]

In reality, the fact that the adumbrations are situated between being and nothingness can be interpreted in an entirely different way: the adumbration would reveal an original mode of being, one more profound than the crude distinction between positive being and negative nothingness, a being-at-a-distance. However, Husserl does not think in accordance with perception but instead interprets adumbrations on the basis of a mode of thought he inherits from the metaphysical tradition, the opposition between being and nothingness. Since being is what surmounts nothingness and can therefore be only an object, givenness by adumbrations, inasmuch as it is not an adequate givenness, represents a threat to the object, throws it on the brink of nothingness. It is clear that the negative dimension of the *époché* particularly emphasized in this text responds to the characterization of what exists as an object; the negation at work in the *époché* is akin to the image of nothingness underlying the positing thesis of the object as a unique mode of possible existence for the world. It is because the world is already reduced to an ensemble of objects that the discord of the adumbrations can prove to be its disappearance and that it therefore becomes possible to posit the hypothesis of the world's annihilation. At this point, it is useless to insist on the unacceptability of this position, which misses precisely the difference between the object and the world: the disappearance of the object not only does not exclude but also reveals the presence of the world as the background against which all objects appear—the presence that, as will be seen, constitutes the true meaning of existence.[24]

It could be argued that the account of reduction in *Ideas I* possesses a completely unique status and that, if the hypothesis of the world's annihilation is evoked, it is only to emphasize the absolute being of lived experience. Husserl always takes care to distinguish the *épochè* from Cartesian doubt. Whereas by denying the world its existence doubt presupposes the sense of being of existence instead of being given the means to inquire into it, the *épochè* suspends the world's existence, places it in brackets, such that the world remains present while the belief that posits it is somehow devitalized. It is indisputable that the *épochè* supposes a certain distance, a form of rupture with the familiar mode of relation to the world in which the latter is given as self-evident, and therefore a suspension of this evidence; in this regard Fink is right to liken it to amazement. However, this distance, taken with respect to our familiar relation to the world characterized by its disappearings in favor of the things that preoccupy or interest us, functions by revealing brute presence, by allowing us to apprehend the "there is" as such. Henceforth, if this distance involves a negative dimension as such, this negation can in no way bear on the world's existence. What is suspended is not the world's existence, but precisely its becoming—the object by means of which its existence as such is concealed. This helps to clarify an enigmatic note by Merleau-Ponty, one of the few that he devotes to reduction:

Wrongly presented—in particular in the *Cartesian Meditations*—as a suspending of the *existence of the world*—If that is what it is, it lapses into a Cartesian defect of being a *hypothesis of the Nichtigkeit of the world*, which immediately has as its consequence the maintenance of the *mens sive anima* (a fragment of the world) as indubitable—Every negation of the world, *but also* every neutrality with regard to the existence of the world, has as its immediate consequence that one misses the transcendental.[25]

In other words, neutralizing the *existence* of the world is taking a position vis-à-vis the *totality* of the world, cutting it out against a background of nothingness, so that such a neutralization can no longer be distinguished from a negation. Whether it involves a suspension or a negation, the attitude that bears on the existence of the world always involves an implicit totalization; therefore it is forced to diminish the sense of being of the world to that of intraworldly being, and it leads necessarily to the positing of a consciousness whose sense of being is identical to that of the neutralized world. Moreover, there is neutrality, respect for the existence of the world—

which is what there is to be understood—only as the negation of what precisely creates an obstacle to focusing on the world as such; there is neutrality only *as the negation of the object* and therefore *of the nothingness it presupposes.* The *épaché* must not take a position on the existence of the world, which would be tantamount to giving it the sense of the object by separating it out against a background of nothingness; on the contrary, it must be given the means of crossing the threshold of the object in order to access this existence that is totally unique, since it is the condition of all existence. The *épaché* distances itself from the world only so as to see the world itself; it is not a distancing from but rather a movement toward the world. In one of the drafts of the chapter titled "Interrogation and Intuition," Merleau-Ponty gives a positive formulation of it, which involves the intertwined rejection of doubt and neutralization: "It [*épaché*] does not break with Being, it does not reduce it to nothingness, does not even disengage itself from it to see it emerge from nothingness, but only puts it in suspense, establishes between it and us a separation in which its relief is visible and in which its silent presence unfolds, which is self-evident, before any thesis."[26]

Nevertheless, we must recognize that Husserl never set forth a definitive formulation of reduction and that the elaboration of its meaning goes hand in hand with the very development of phenomenology. Thus Husserl becomes gradually conscious of the difficulties associated with the Cartesian approach and attempts to develop other means of accessing the transcendental that would not be encumbered by the difficulties that were pointed out in the foregoing. The risk lies in confusion between the natural attitude and the naturalistic attitude, in determination of the world of our spontaneous life according to the categories that govern scientific activity, among the first of which figures the category of the pure object.[27] It is therefore necessary to proceed to an initial reduction that suspends the idealizations of knowledge—scientific knowledge in particular—in order to establish the pregiven world that constitutes its foundation; such is the project of *The Crisis of European Sciences and Transcendental Phenomenology.* It is easy to demonstrate that Husserl does not succeed in realizing this project, in determining a sense of being of the world that is truly independent of the idealizations to which it gives rise. The life-world possesses, as Husserl puts it, the same structures as those presupposed by the objective sciences; it is not so much determined on the basis of itself as on the possibility of accounting for the objectifying activity of science. It follows from this that the world is defined as "the universe of things, which are distributed within the world-form of space-time and are 'positional' in two senses (according to spatial position and temporal position)—the spatio-temporal *onta*."[28]

It is therefore not surprising that this first reduction to the life world is followed by a second reduction that constitutes this world at the center of transcendental subjectivity. Because he does not proceed to the specific figure of this world, because he clings to the determination of its sense of being as an object, Husserl grasps it by starting with the possibility of resolving its facticity in a givenness of meaning. This is why Merleau-Ponty is right to submit the return to the life world to a determinate alternative. Either it is a question of a return to the world as such, in keeping its own appearance (in which case any constitution within a transcendental subjectivity would be inconceivable) or such a constitution can be envisioned, but that would mean that the life world is still an objective world, that its specificity is missed, and that the initial reduction has failed.

3

The Three Moments of Appearance

The *époché* is a method that affords access to the sense of being of the world and cannot be an act of suspension of the world's existence; it is the destruction of the obstacles that compromise the apprehension of this existence as such, according to its true sense. These obstacles can be summed up in the attitude that consists in suspending this existence in nothingness and then determining it as an object. The *époché* therefore becomes the *negation of nothingness* in order to root out the prejudice regarding the object and to give access to the sense of being of what is. Thus characterized, it appears as the inverse of the version thematized by Husserl: the *époché* does not lead from the suspension of the world to the thing as constituted in consciousness; rather, it leads *from suspension of the thing, via negation of nothingness, to recognition of the world.*

Now, what is the exact residuum of this reduction? What does it enable one to gain in relation to Husserl's transcendental reduction? To deny pure nothingness as the preliminary condition of being is to recognize a "reality" always already there as constitutive of appearance, an originary foundation that essentially cannot be denied since it is the preliminary basis required by any negation. In other words, to deny nothingness is equivalent to recognizing that there is manifestation only on the basis of an all-encompassing totality and therefore that it is incapable of being totalized, a totality that includes—in advance, so to speak—all that can emerge; it is the originary fact that does not actualize any essence but, on the contrary, is the foundation of any essence, because it is the basis of all that is conceivable.

The discovery of the impossibility of nothingness is simultaneously the revelation of a being that cannot not be, in the sense that it is foreign to negation, that always predates what emerges in it, and that therefore plays the role of originary possibility for any effective reality. The negation of nothingness leads us therefore to what is both most evident and most difficult to conceive of: that "there is" something. It functions indeed as a reduction in that it allows one to see this "there is" as such; to approach being without an interposed nothingness is to approach appearance without an interposed object, in its autonomy. Whereas the residuum of the *époché* conceived of as the suspension of the world was consciousness giving meaning, the residuum of an *époché* as the negation of nothingness is the certainty of an originary "there is," a necessary condition for any manifestation. From the discovery of the impossibility of nothingness, the *époché* brings to light a field of presence necessarily preliminary to any manifestation whatsoever; it is thereby the unveiling disclosure *of the structure of belonging that is constitutive of appearance*. To say that pure nothingness is impossible and that negativity always supposes being is to recognize that there is manifestation only within or on the basis of an encompassing reality. However, this inscription in an encompassing reality does not correspond to a factual relation between beings; rather, it designates *an essential determination of the manifestation*. Appearance is always appearance in the midst of something else, which is why the encompassing itself does not appear. If it could be otherwise, the result would be a reality that is not enveloped by any other, that as absolutely closed, therefore has nothingness outside of itself, which contradicts the refusal of nothingness that underlies the reduction at hand. It can therefore be seen that this approach to appearance is the exact opposite of the one examined earlier. If a conception of manifestation as susceptible to an adequate determination is underpinned by the preliminary positing of nothingness, then it is clear that a critique of this nothingness will lead one to consider as constitutive of the manifestation its insertion in a milieu on the basis of which the very horizon of adequacy becomes devoid of meaning. If it is true that the being-inscribed-in or the being-in-the-midst-of is the constitutive characteristic of appearance, then the closure of the object must be abandoned and an essential continuity between manifestation and its field must be admitted.

Moreover, to say that belonging is constitutive of appearance is tantamount to recognizing that *the world, too, is constitutive of manifestation*. Appearance is always appearance within the world; any manifestation of something is in principle a *comanifestation of a world*. Indeed, the world is this open totality, this encompassing absolute, a field for all possible events. It is neither the sum of beings that emerge there nor a sort of super object, whether we conceive of it as an empty framework or as a specific environment independent of what appears, but instead the vital force of any manifestation, an element that is not distinguished from it, precisely because it is not an object, an element that is therefore none other than the ensemble of manifestations and is constituted at the same time as they are. As Patočka writes: "The world is not sum, but preliminary totality. We cannot set ourselves outside the world, raise ourselves above it. The world is, by all its being, *midst*, in contrast with what it is the midst of. For this reason, it is never object. For this same reason, it is unique, indivisible. Any division, any individuation is *in the world*, but has no meaning for the world."[1]

It is now easier to understand why it was important to exhaust this approach, to approach the world from the structure of belonging that is itself revealed by reduction. It is not a question of positing an all-encompassing structure, one that is somehow preliminary and would justify the structure of the inscription of each being; to take this approach would be to relapse, albeit in a more sophisticated way, into the ontology of the object. The all-encompassing of the world is rigorously the reverse of belonging as the essence of appearance; the world as well as the appearing are derived from this essential structure as its constitutive moments. It is not because there is a world that all manifestations are manifestations in the midst of something else; it is, on the contrary, because belonging is part of the essence of appearance that *the manifestation of something is always at the same time a manifestation of a world*. Be that as it may, the residuum of *épochè* as it was just defined is precisely the world itself. What is discovered as absolute or as apodictic, as implicated essentially by any manifestation, is not consciousness but rather this totality. Appearance is not initially appearance to a consciousness; it is appearance within a world. To say that belonging constitutes the essence of appearance is tantamount to recognizing that any reduction to nothingness, whatever it may be, leaves the existence of the world intact. To affirm that nothingness does not precede being, that being does not stand out against a background of nothingness, is to understand that the negation of the world itself *still presupposes the existence of the world* and thus reveals its unquestionableness; it is a contradictory act. Such is exactly the significance of the essential character of what we called the structure of belonging. The world is the a priori of appearance because belonging is its constitutive structure. As Patočka writes, more insightfully than anyone previously in attempting to thematize this a priori of the world:

There must be a unique connection at the interior of which is everything that *there is.* This *unique* connection is in the strict sense what is. Taken from the point of view of what we have already said, it is the condition of all experiences. However, it is also the condition of all particular beings in their particular being. *Thus, the form-of-the-world (Weltform) of experience is also what makes an experience of the world possible.* This all-encompassing being unique, it follows that it must *always* be there as the permanent backdrop to experience. This also implies that there cannot be two totalities of being and, therefore, that experience as experience of being is necessarily concordant.[2]

Once the reduction has been effected, the object of our wonder appears as the opposite of a thesis. It cannot proceed from an act, being what is presupposed by all acts; no "I" can perform it since the world it posits as all-encompassing contains it too. Rather, it corresponds to the dimension of passivity inherent in any thesis—corresponds to the foundation it always requires inasmuch as it cannot be a pure creation, does not spring from nothingness, and in this regard is an opinion or originary belief (*Urglaube, Urdoxa*). This particular positing of the world "is manifested, among others, in that transcendence (intentional, immanent) as such can *never be constituted,* that it is, in any constitution, already presupposed as being the general foundation. Moreover, to the degree that this foundation is never constructed, it precisely does *not* belong to the intra-worldly experimented singular."[3]

The *époché* allows us to liberate the structure of the appearance from the fullness of the appearing object and thus reestablish its autonomy. The essence of appearance implies a relation to a basis or field of manifestation; it is characterized by envelopment, by belonging, and this is why it contains a relation of the appearing with the whole of the world.[4] It must therefore be admitted that the appearance of any appearing whatsoever implies, in a way that remains to be determined, the comanifestation of the world. From this perspective, one could object that the determination of appearance is again dependent on an appearing. However, this dependence has a completely different meaning from the one criticized earlier regarding the object, because this appearing is nothing but the world itself. The comanifestation of the world in any manifestation is by no means reduced to the presence of a content, a being that would presuppose appearance. As the basis of all appearing, the world is in a sense certainly a content; it must be pregiven if anything is to be given. But as the basis of *all* content, it is capable of containing everything, and in a sense it is the opposite of content. As the pregiven of everything given, it can have no other content than that which is given in it; it has for its only content capacity itself, and in this regard it moves toward form. As the originary unity of a given and a condition of givenness, the world is the identity of form and content, or rather their indifference. On the one hand, it cannot be likened to a form since, quite the contrary, it is the ultimate appearing; it corresponds to what in each manifestation does not appear, the unpresentable and inexhaustible dimension of each presentation. The world is unformed because it is the basis of all giving of form, the basis for all representation, predating any synthesis or structure. On the other hand, it is also foreign to the order of content since it is the field in which a content can appear, in which every content emerges; if the world is indeed self-contained, it can under no circumstances be situated within the contained. It must be remembered that its co-givenness is required by the constitutive structure of belonging proper to appearance. The world is always presupposed by any manifestation because it is what can contain any appearing; it is therefore both the ultimate given and the final condition. One can say that it is indistinctly what is manifested by each appearing thing, as the depth it brings to appearance and the condition of its manifestation. It is the obscurity from which the spark of manifestation emerges and at the same time what gives the manifestation its spark. Each manifestation is *of* the world, both in the sense of capacity and initiative. This is also why the world avoids the opposition between activity and passivity; deeper than any act inasmuch as it constitutes the latter's basis, the world produces the manifestation since, as realized belonging, it realizes its condition of appearance. Thus, as a constituent in the chemical sense, just as in the philosophical sense, the world is the originary identity of the ontological and the transcendental. This appearing that is constitutive of appearance therefore has by no means the status of the appearings whose manifestation it allows. It is the ultimate condition of manifestation because it is the ultimate encompassing for all appearing; it never appears itself.

The result of this is that the perplexity arising when one is faced with an appearance whose essence refers to a transcendent appearing (in reality to transcendence itself, which is a synonym for the world) is rooted in an attitude consisting of identifying appearance as such with a subjective provision and of situating it thereby toward form. Moreover, the analysis of appearance being developed here results precisely in a total abolition of the undue privilege of the "subjective" and thus represents the most radical refutation of this "transcendentalist" attitude. The determination of the essence of appearance as belonging is equally valid for any appearance whatsoever, *even for this extraordinary appearance of the human person to itself called consciousness.* The appearance of the subject (the name commonly given to the human person as the being for whom there is manifestation) to itself is subject to the general conditions of appearance, to the givenness of a world; the manifestation of my own existence, my consciousness, has as its basis and condition the originary manifestation of the world.

The Husserlian perspective is thoroughly inverted here. Whereas the latter postulates an eidetic abyss between two modes of being—consciousness and natural reality—an abyss that was strictly based on their specific mode of appearance, without adumbrations and by adumbrations, respectively, the point of view adopted here leads one to posit a univocal sense of appearance: appearance is one, whatever the nature of the appearing and therefore of the manifestation. It involves insertion into a field, envelopment by the world, and consequently a form of depth that arises insofar as each manifestation is inscribed and as retained in the world it manifests. If all manifestations are simultaneously of a world as untotalizable totality, appearing cannot be fully present in its manifestation, and the latter is therefore characterized by a sort of obscurity or distance—which is not the inverse of a possible proximity since it is merely the expression of appearing's being-in-the-world.

Moreover, this is equally true for the subject's manifestation to itself. Insofar as it requires the manifestation of a world and is inscribed in this manifestation, it also involves a dimension of distance or obscurity and therefore enjoys no privilege vis-à-vis the manifestation of the thing. In other words, if one admits that this comanifestation of the world in all manifestations is nothing more than the ultimate justification of what Husserl recognized in the concept of givenness by adumbrations, then one must say that lived experience *is given by adumbrations* just as the thing is. One understands by this that one is never present oneself in manifestations; that the subject, no more than the thing, is not given in an adequate way in its lived experiences, meaning in reality in an experience of itself that is shown to consist strictly speaking in a certain relationship to the world.

Thus the implemented *épochè* has consequences contrary to those it has in Husserl. It does not extend to the order of immanence, in which a coincidence of self with self would be achieved and therefore an apodicticity that is lacking in the experience of the object; on the contrary, it undoes the order of immanence, dispossesses consciousness of itself and therefore of its founding pretension. It truly involves an *époché without reduction*, an elucidation of appearance in its autonomy and consequently as independent in relation to subjective manifestation. As Patočka points out, "What is 'discovered as already there,' what *emerges*, is not what is absolute as 'immanent *datum*,' but the '*trans*' (*das 'darüber hinaus'*), what *contrasts the coincidence* of the intuitioned with the intuitioning in always referring beyond and in always being beyond the given."[5]

Thus, whereas in Husserl the appearance of the world has as a priori the appearance of consciousness to itself—the manifestation of a certain appearing—the *époché* being thematized here liberates the autonomy of appearance vis-à-vis any manifestation and leads to affirming that the world, insofar as it is constitutive of appearance, *is the a priori of the manifestation of the subject to itself, of consciousness.* Far from the notion that the world is constituted in lived experiences, there are lived experiences only on the basis of the world. This remarkable relation to the self called consciousness has as a condition relation to the world: manifestation of the self, inasmuch as it is initially a manifestation, presupposes the originary manifestation of the world, which is why the self, like the object, is characterized by a constitutive invisibility.[6] Thus *époché* not only leads to the criticism of the so-called abyss separating consciousness from reality by reestablishing the univocity of appearance, it also reverses the relation of subordination that Husserl thematized, such that reality has priority over consciousness. Priority is given back to the depths of the world implied by appearance, and consciousness proceeds from it and is as subordinated to the manifestation of the world, insofar as consciousness is caught up in the structure of appearance. As Patočka remarks, it is necessary to think "not of appearance as such as something subjective, but on the contrary, of the subjective as a 'realization' of the structure of manifestation. . . . Appearance has the particularity of being an interiorization of the universe, of having the universe as its very subject, simply using concrete subjects to be realized, however being in itself a generally universal structure, *being the universe itself* in its depths and originality."[7]

It is this structure of appearance—inasmuch as it implies the manifestation of a world that never appears in person and therefore leads to a dimension of invisibility, that is constitutive of any vision—that Merleau-

Ponty calls "flesh" in his working notes. It is, he writes, "the Being-seen, i.e. is a Being that is *eminently percipi*, and it is by it that we can understand the *percipere*; . . . all this is finally possible and means something only because *there is* Being, not Being in itself, identical to itself, in the night, but the Being that also contains its negation, its *percipi*."[8]

Nevertheless, in subordinating consciousness of the self to the general structure of appearance, the subject is not reduced to insignificance; nor is any specificity in relation to other appearings denied to it. Clearly the autonomy of appearance cannot be understood as the autosubsistence of a being, nor therefore as an anonymous manifestation that would not imply constitutively someone *to whom* this appears. Indeed, it must be said that if the essence of appearance implies the manifestation of a world, the essence of this world implies that it cannot be distinguished from its manifestation. If it is true, as Patočka states, that appearance is the universe itself, it must be added that this universe is its appearance—in accordance with this unity of the *esse* and the *percipi* that Merleau-Ponty thematizes—and that this universe therefore cannot be conceived of without reference to a "who" to whom it appears. In short, the fact that the subject (the one to whom the universe appears) is not a constituent part of the world but, on the contrary, is dependent on appearance as manifestation of a world does not rule out but rather implies that this subject is equally constitutive of this structure inasmuch as there is appearance of the world only as appearance *for*. To say that the world is constitutive of appearance is to say that in every being the world appears and that every being is therefore essentially linked to a subject to whom this world appears. It should be added right away, even though it will be developed more fully in the following chapters, that the specificity of the subject in relation to other beings depends precisely on the fact of its reflecting the comanifestation of the world in each manifestation, that as a subject of the world it is capable of relating to an untotalizable totality. The distance inherent in the test of self and the dispossession that characterizes the subject respond precisely to the irremediable withdrawal from the world in each manifestation. In contrast to Husserl, for whom the figure of the world must be constituted on the basis of the composition of the subject, it is the structure of the world that serves as the thread leading to the characterization of this subject.

Whichever the case—the subject is not constitutive of the world or the world is the constitutive basis of appearance—this does not prevent the reference to a subject from being part of the very structure of appearance.

Thus "the fundamental law of appearance, is that there is always the duality between *what* appears and *to what* this appearing appears. It is not the *to what* the appearing appears that *creates* the manifestation, that *effectuates* it, 'constitutes' it, produces it in whatever way. On the contrary, appearance is appearance only in this duality" so that "the phenomenon, the appearance, has as moments what appears (the world), what the appearing appears to (subjectivity) and the *how*, the way in which the appearing appears."[9]

In other words, if the world as appearing refers essentially to a subjective perspective, this does not mean that what appears is a simple image of the world, nor even that the world is constituted as such by the subject; the subject stands in relation to the world *itself*. The world being, the reality of the world, implies its appearance and therefore its reference to a subjective pole, but this reference by no means involves any interiorization whatsoever. As was pointed out earlier without having been justified, phenomenality does not exclude "objectivity," transcendence. Strictly speaking, appearance signifies the very presence of the thing according to a certain point of view, which is why the distinction between the hyletic moment and its corresponding objective moment is devoid of meaning. The world refers indeed to a subject, but the subject cannot in any way relate to the transcendent through lived experiences. The lived experience is an illusory phenomenon, whose critique demands elucidation of the subject's specific mode of existence.

It must be remembered that belonging characterizes the essence of manifestation and that therefore the subject for whom there is a world *is itself part of the world*; this is the reason its participation in the manifestation of the world cannot imply any interiorization or constitution whatsoever. The subject does not escape from the law of manifestation that the inscription in the world imposes upon it; in keeping with the image of the brain in Bergson's work, the subject does not contain the world but is contained in it. The assertion that the subject is dependent on appearance must therefore be understood in two ways. On the one hand, it means that far from being the source of appearance the subject is a moment of it, just as the world is a moment of it; it is because there is initially a phenomenon that there is simultaneously an appearing world and a subject to whom it appears. On the other hand, it means, by virtue of the fundamental insertion of all appearing in the world, that the subject for whom there is a world is also part of the world. This is tantamount to saying that the subject of appearance *is essentially incarnated*, that the incarnation is demanded by the structure of phenomenality just articulated. It is not because one is incarnated that one has a point of view on the world; rather, it is because the essence of phenomenality implies that the subject to whom the world appears be inscribed in it that one is incarnated. One's inscription in the world, which is realized as a body, is merely the consequence of the structure of any manifestation's constitutive belonging. One's incarnation is a characteristic of phenomenality.

It is easy to see that the whole difficulty now consists in elucidating the very event of manifestation, the strictly "subjective" moment of appearance that is tantamount to attempting to understand how a being that is part of the world can be the subject of appearance. Insofar as it is involved in the structure of appearance, it is clear that the subject does not constitute the world, nor even represent it to itself in any way; the subject relates itself to the world. It is nevertheless true that it is not just one being among other beings and does not experience the world in an objective and causal mode; it is not the manifestation that produces in the subject images or lived experiences.[10] One could say that the subject *conditions* the manifestation in the sense that it does not cause it, but neither is it subject to it. The subject therefore possesses a structure whereby the appearance of the world can pass through it and whereby phenomenality can be actualized. However, to the degree that it is a moment of appearance, there is no question whatsoever of asking how it can produce or give birth to a manifestation; all we may claim is to reveal its characteristic mode of being as it is *adapted* to the structure of appearance, as it can be integrated in it. Hence, the approach to the subject's mode of being must immediately dispense with any recourse to something as lived experience; rather, the originary mode of being to which the phenomenon deceptively characterized as lived refers must be clarified. The *percipere* is what is made possible by the *percipi*, and therefore wanting to approach the *percipere* as the source of the *percipi* makes no sense. "There is" appearance, "there is" a world, and the question is knowing what the mode of being of perceiving is and therefore in what perception consists, as the conditioning moment of the structure of manifestation.[11] Before confronting this question, it is thus necessary first of all to characterize more precisely this structure of manifestation, the *how* that constitutes the third moment of appearance.

The characterization developed thus far of the structure of appearance still remains abstract. Any manifestation implies the comanifestation of the world, such that the world itself is manifested in all appearing. But *how* is the appearing given if it is precisely comanifestation of the world? How is the world itself given in each appearing? How is this originary relation manifested, this cobelonging of each appearing being and the world? The givenness of the world in each manifestation is derived from the structure of belonging that is constitutive of appearance. Moreover, to what mode of specific presence does this structure of belonging correspond? In other words, what is the concrete form of the experience of the a priori?

To answer these questions, it is necessary to return to our point of departure, Bergson's critique of nothingness, on the basis of which we have attempted to elaborate a new formulation of reduction. Thus far only the negative aspect of Bergson's analysis has been presented: the critique of the principle of sufficient reason and therefore the rejection of the illusory character of the essentialist conceptions of the being deriving from that principle. Now, it appears that the critique of nothingness as the background from which being must be wrested is not equivalent to a rejection without nuances of the negative; on the contrary, it implies recognition of a specific form of negativity. What is excluded by the reduction as it has been formulated here relying on Bergson's works *is not nothingness itself so much as its "positivity,"* the massive opposition between a nothingness that would be completely negative and a fully positive being. The essentialist or "positivist" conception of being arose because it was approached on the basis of nothingness, on the presupposition of the possible existence of a pure nothingness that would envelop it.

Thus the critique of the illusory character of this positing compels one to question the pure positivity of being. To approach being directly, without passing through nothingness, is to discover in it *a dimension of negativity* since its positive fullness was precisely justified only by the positing of this preliminary nothingness. The positivity of being responds exactly to the negativity of nothingness from which it is set off, in denying the latter, consequently abandoning the former. We must therefore introduce negativity into the very definition of being, a negativity whose meaning is naturally entirely different from that of the pure nothingness that was denied. Hence, far from being equivalent to the exclusion of any negative dimension, the critique of pure nothingness opens a path to an adequate determination of nothingness as the interior dimension of being; it ultimately allows an inquiry into *the negative's sense of being.* The naïveté that was shown to be at the root of objectivism causes one to miss the true sense of being of what is because it is initially naïveté in regard to the sense of being of nothingness itself.

In conceiving of nothingness as what is thoroughly negative and therefore is necessarily less than being, it refuses even to pose the question concerning its own sense of being. On the contrary, to deny positing of a preliminary nothingness in the name of the phenomenological naïveté of this decision is to discover that one cannot separate the question of the sense of the being of what is from an inquiry into the sense of being of nothingness. Thus in rejecting nothingness as an autonomous "reality" preliminary to being, the reduction is forced to accept it in the form of a constitutive negativity of being, an originary weakness or an originary indeterminacy that distinguishes it precisely from a pure object. To abandon the positivity of the negative is ipso facto to accept the negativity of the positive. It must be understood in the strict sense; it is not a question of a dimension that would be added to being or that would carve out its constitutive density,[12] but of a negativity that is *constitutive of being itself,* that is inherent in appearance. By means of reduction, the exteriority and mutual exclusion of being and nothingness are transformed into a profound unity, into a fusion more originary than the terms involved. The alterity of the positive and the negative gives way to an immediate identity: *it is as positive that the positive is negative,* which is tantamount to saying that the presence of the appearing involves essentially a dimension of indeterminacy or retreat.[13]

It is true that Bergson does not arrive at this conclusion, at least not in the text in which he develops the critique of nothingness, and that he demonstrates a certain inconsistency. This is explained by the context of this critique. Because his intention is thereby to rehabilitate duration in its ontological positivity, he emphasizes the fact that being, cut out against a background of nothingness, is characterized by immutability, an indifference to becoming. Henceforth, in refusing to rely on the principle of sufficient reason, Bergson rehabilitates becoming as a complete reality and thus transfers to duration the ontological positivity that metaphysics accorded to essence. In so doing, he does not thematize the fact that it is by virtue of its positivity that being resists nothingness, that its indifference to becoming is a consequence of its fullness of determination. It is precisely this fullness that the critique of nothingness is intended to "decompress," so that if this critique results in a rehabilitation of duration it also requires that a dimension of negativity be recognized in it.[14] Because the immutable essence resists nothingness by virtue of its positivity, the ever-changing reality that his critique allows to be discovered is necessarily permeated by negativity. As Lebrun points out: "Bergson recognizes undoubtedly that true mobility—

duration—is the difference with self, however it is for making it achieve substantial dignity that Hegel praises Zenon for having freed movement. Bergsonianism is therefore less a critique of metaphysics than a displacement of its subject: Being has only changed content."[15]

Thus Bergson's critique of nothingness, in which we have seen the beginning of an authentic phenomenological reduction, indicates to us, in a way a contrario, how to characterize the residuum of reduction, the sense of being of being approached without interposed nothingness. This is certainly what Merleau-Ponty was attempting by means of a parallel meditation contrasting Bergson's and Husserl's philosophies, which is confirmed by several late, unpublished notes; he remarks for example, in February 1959, that "Bergson is correct in his critique of nothingness. His error is only in neither saying nor seeing that the being that obdurates nothingness is not being." The residuum of the reduction must be understood as "something" inasmuch as it is different from the fully determinable thing; it is "not nothing," not in the sense that it surmounts a preliminary nothingness but in the sense that it always precedes it and constitutes the basis upon which a negativity can emerge. The "there is" is this gentle or tacit presence that, because it does not negate nothingness, never attains the full determination of the object. It is not nothing and nothing more, the declared impossibility of the ontological void. The mode of existing liberated by the reduction thus conceived is the immediate identity between the positive and the negative; its manifestation, its phenomenal positivity is accompanied by a kind of interior distance.

It follows from this analysis that the structure of belonging by which we have initially characterized phenomenality must be given to us in a form in which an identity between the positive and the negative is affirmed, or rather in a form in which their very distinction is seen as abolished. This structure that is constitutive of appearance includes the idea that nothing can be given if the world, as the field or basis of this manifestation, is not itself given, so that the givenness of any thing presupposes the *originary* givenness of the world. Originarity in the sense that Husserl understands it, as "originary giving intuition," or as perception that gives the thing "in the flesh," itself refers to a more profound sense of originarity that corresponds to the givenness of the world as preliminary to and condition of any manifestation. Moreover, the world cannot be given *itself* since it is an all-encompassing totality. Its manifestation would mean its disappearance to the degree that this manifestation would be possible only on the basis of world; the world can never be encountered because every encounter assumes the possibility of a nonencounter or an avoiding. It follows that originarity not only allows but implies a dimension of absence so that at the level of the originary givenness of the world perception can in no way coincide with fullness as the fulfillment of emptiness.[16] Quite the contrary, as the matrix of originary presence the presence of the world *reveals a cobelonging, itself originary, of emptiness and fulfillment, of absence and presence.*

To say that the world is originarily given is to recognize that emptiness, which is inherent in the absence of the world as such, is a mode of the given.[17] In other words, one finds clarified here Husserl's hesitation between a characterization of perception as givenness in the flesh, which accepts lacunae, and its determination as fullness, as fulfillment of the empty intentionality, an adequate grasp conforming to the ideal of reason. Instead of defining the originarity by the presence of the thing itself, ultimately by intuition, we must, on the contrary, define presence and intuition on the basis of originary givenness as givenness of a world. It turns out, then, that presence necessarily implies a dimension of nonpresence, that intuition is inevitably intertwined with the nonintuitive. Even while recognizing that the thing itself is given by adumbrations, Husserl maintains the horizon of an adequate givenness of the object, such that this absence of the thing in its adumbrations is ultimately regarded as an "imperfection", a lack of presence. Quite the contrary, once it is understood that what is given originarily is none other than the world as untotalizable totality, absence no longer appears as negation, but as a condition of presence. In this context, it is only a question of recognizing the presence of the world behind the givenness of the thing, instead of emphasizing the constitution of the thing on the basis of a suspension of the world. If everything is a thing *of the world* since it can appear only within a world and therefore its perception assumes its originary givenness, one must consequently abandon the horizon of adequacy and understand that the nonpresentation of the thing in the adumbration is the condition of its manifestation, that the distance from the thing is only the reverse of its phenomenal proximity. An adequate perception of the object would require the clarification of its basis of belonging, of the roots it grows in the world, its "exterior horizons." Requiring a totalization of the infinite, it is equivalent to a contradiction pure and simple. Reality is perceived only at a distance; the separation of the adumbration vis-à-vis the thing is not the expression of our finitude but a constitutive characteristic of appearance.

Thus, insofar as it assumes an originary givenness of the world and the world is what cannot in principle be completely given, the structure of belonging that characterizes appearance is given as the presence of what can only be absent, as the presentation of something unpresentable. Such is the sense of this immediate unity of the positive and the negative to which our critique of nothingness opened upon. The test of belonging that is implied in any experience assumes that the manifestation is seized as a negation even though that of which it is the negation cannot be attained positively, as if the negative and incomplete character that typifies manifestation were simultaneously the positing of what it negates, as if the absence of what appears were its own manner of being present. I grasp the manifestation as a manifestation *of something*; I am certain of being able to continue the experience triggered by this manifestation even though I miss the thing of which it is the experience. Although the thing is not given to me, the fact that this manifestation is a manifestation of the thing is given to me; I can continue the flow of the experience "that I have once again, wherever I am, the possibility of achieving the same continuation, this is not simply anticipated, but *given* in the form, not of a simple intention, but of a contingent *independent* presence or of a simple empty anticipation."[18]

Otherwise stated, this infinite flow of the adumbrations in which the givenness of the thing as it is in itself would consist, and to which Husserl referred to as an idea in the Kantian sense, is effectively *given*; what Husserl considered to be a regulator must in reality be understood as *constitutive*. The fact that the object cannot be given to me itself from the moment that, as an object of the world, it envelops the infinite *is itself given to me*. The infinite flow that separates the present manifestation from the appearing object and whose extension coincides with the totality of the world is present to me in person. Truly it is from this presence of the infinite, or rather from the infinite as presence, that the object and its present manifestation are conjointly given to me with respect to their identity and their difference; inasmuch as the infinite is present to me, the manifestation is given as a manifestation *of something*. However, inasmuch as this presence is the presence of the infinite, it is given as being *only a manifestation*. We can therefore understand from this specific presence how the object can be present in the adumbration while being infinitely distanced from it, how the adumbration can give rise to the object while delaying its full presence. The possibility of appearance—as originary unity of a presence and an absence, a distance and a proximity—relies on the givenness of the infinite itself, which is why the evidence to which Husserl appeals, "according to which this infinity cannot in principle be given," is quite simply false evidence. On the contrary, there is evidence, thus perceptual presence, only on the basis of the givenness of this infinity. So inasmuch as it originarily envelops the manifestation of the world, the essence of appearance consists in the givenness of an infinite that separates and brings together each manifestation with what appears in it; it relies on *the givenness in person of the impossibility to be given exhaustively.*

The concept of *horizon* names this singular appearance, this givenness of the constitutive unpresentable nature of the manifestation inasmuch as it is the comanifestation of a world; *horizon(t)ality is the concrete form of the experience of the a priori.*[19] The constitutive belonging of appearance is not grasped as a relation between terms preliminarily given; as has been seen, both the originary givenness of the world and the finite manifestation proceed from the structure of belonging and constitute its internal moments. Therefore, belonging must be attained by itself; there must be a test for the constitutive structure of appearance. A horizon is the locus of this test. It designates the being-in-the-world of the appearing, the shift of all manifestation toward a pole forever absent, which manifestation indicates without ever presenting it itself and which constitutes it as a manifestation. The horizon is the test of this excess or this retreat into the self that characterizes any presence insofar as it takes root in the originary givenness of the world. The consciousness of horizon, Patočka writes, is "a preliminary, not thematic, knowledge based on the encompassing One that in all singular knowledge is present as project on the basis of forgetfulness, and that, where it is focused, disguises itself initially as continuation of the singular experience."[20] However, it must be added immediately that by virtue of the way in which it is defined here the horizon cannot refer to a consciousness.

Because Husserl maintains the pole of an exhaustive givenness (or, the equivalent, because he remains a prisoner of the punctuality of sensory presence, thus missing the constitutive surpassing of the adumbration), he refers the horizon to a consciousness; because the absence of the object in the adumbration can refer only to a delayed presence, what is distinguished from the punctuality of the adumbration without being merged with the object can have only the status of a subjective anticipation. From the moment that the idea of an adequate donation is maintained, the distance that separates the manifestation from it cannot be conceived of as a mode of constitutive being. It therefore finds itself ultimately referred to as a "potentiality of consciousness." Moreover, to understand that any manifestation is originarily a manifestation of the world is to realize that the absence of the object is irreducible, because it is none other than the untotalizable infinity of its adumbrations. But it is also to understand that from this infinity, ultimately from this absence, there is a specific givenness in the form of horizon. Thus horizon is not supported by consciousness; on the contrary, it is consciousness insofar as it is consciousness of something that assumes a horizon. Merleau-Ponty is therefore correct when he writes, "No more than are the sky or the earth is the horizon a collection of slender* things, or a class name, or a logical possibility of conception, or a system of 'potentiality of conscious'; it is a new type of being."[21]

It is this "new type of being" that allows one to account for the possibility of perception as "givenness by adumbrations." As has been seen, perception is characterized by the fact that the manifestation conceals the object while revealing it, that the object appears only while remaining absent from what presents it. This is why we can speak of adumbration in the sense in which the adumbration, insofar as it is *only* an adumbration, is also an elusion from the object that it gives. Husserl does not pursue this fundamental intuition once he conceives of what is adumbrated as a pure object that is in itself determinable, and thereby he shifts the adumbration to the subjective point of view, turning it into a punctual lived experience. Moreover, we perceive now that this givenness by adumbrations refers to the specific structure of appearance, and that it cannot be compounded; therefore it is reconstituted. It is first of all clear that it is impossible to account for perception by starting with an act of consciousness and that there is therefore access to perception only on the basis of a conjoined reduction of objective and subjective existence. Thus it is necessary to recognize the autonomy of appearance vis-à-vis all, even subjective, appearing; far from it constituting the order of the perceived, perception is possible only on the basis of perceived being as autonomous being.

The reference to a subject is part of the structure of appearance, but it does not exhaust the essence of the latter. To the contrary, what description gathers under the heading of "givenness by adumbrations" refers to the constitutive structure of appearance insofar as it is the originary manifestation of a world—refers, that is, to the structure of horizon. Horizon designates this rooting of the manifestation in something invisible that it presents in its invisibility, this excess beyond the self that is constitutive of the manifestation insofar as it is the comanifestation of a world. The structure of the horizon names the fact that the manifestation is always more than itself, that it therefore develops a depth presented in it only as its own absence, that it conceals in the very act by which it reveals. This is tantamount to saying that the givenness by adumbrations that characterizes perception takes root in the structure of the horizon; the act of adumbrating that gives meaning to the notion of adumbration is the work of the horizon. To conceive of appearance as structured according to a horizon is to think of adumbrating as being.[22]

One can account for perception only on the condition that one fully recognize the autonomy of appearance in relation to appearing, because horizon escapes the laws of formal ontology that govern the appearing object in general. The structure of the horizon reveals a mode of being that defies the principle of identity. As reference to an untotalizable totality, it is greater than itself; it opens onto an alterity that, insofar as it becomes invisible in it, it is not distinct from identity. It is given as the identity of itself and its other.[23] One would therefore need to deploy a formal ontology in a particular sense, an ontology that would attempt to describe the very logic of appearance insofar as it is manifestly different from the logic of appearing. It is without question Merleau-Ponty who developed this distinction to the fullest, and a number of the working notes for *The Visible and the Invisible* can be considered as examples of this ontology. It is clear that such an ontology cannot be explained by means of ordinary language, in which all the laws of formal ontology are buried, and that it therefore requires the elaboration of a new language and new concepts, which are judged to be metaphorical only on the basis of a false idea of metaphor and of ontology itself.

It follows from this that all perceived subjects are characterized by a constitutive distance. To affirm that appearance is essentially appearance in a horizon is to recognize that there is presence only when it is retained in the depths of the world it reveals. Because it is greater than itself, the perceived subject draws back under the gaze and sinks into a distance that is not the opposite of a possible proximity, for it is synonymous with the untotalizable character of the world that appears in it. Insofar as the perceived is an excess beyond or a withdrawal from the self, its distance does not refer to a relation, to a reducible separation in relationship to a "here"; rather, it constitutes its mode of being. If it is true, as Merleau-Ponty writes, "that to see is always to see more than one sees,"[24] then it must be admitted that the seen remains always withdrawn from its manifestation and therefore that its transcendence is constitutive of its phenomenality.

We suggest calling the phenomenal order thus constituted sensible. It is time to abandon the distinction between sensation and perception. This distinction, which dominates Husserl's analysis of givenness by adumbrations, includes the opposition between presence strictly speaking and the object that, though present in person, is not however given as it is in itself. To say regarding a reality that it is given in the flesh, that it is effectively present, is to say that it is given to me in sensations, and this is why one can distinguish from this mode of givenness the perceptual presence in which the object is not integrally present, in the sense that it is not given to me completely on a sensory basis. Thus Husserl's analysis is unquestionably determined by the classic opposition between sensation that gives the only presence (existence) and perception that gives the object whose existence it is (and on this basis requires the intervention of the mind in one form or another). Otherwise stated, Husserl equates the sensible with the originary, but he subordinates it immediately to the empiricist concept of sensation. By contrast, it is proposed to suspend the apparent evidence of the concept of the sensible and to conceptualize it *on the basis of the originary*. Moreover, the nature of originary givenness, insofar as it is the givenness of a world, is precisely that it involves a dimension of invisibility or transcendence that the concept of horizon names.

Beyond the abstract distinction between sensation and object, the sensible therefore designates the element in which something can appear insofar as this thing remains veiled in its appearance, insofar as the transcendence of what appears is preserved in it. The sensible is nothing more than what can appear without being posited and therefore involves a tacit or implicit dimension. It maintains a kind of opaqueness at the very heart of its luminosity; this is why one experiences it simultaneously as evident and impenetrable. As Merleau-Ponty expresses it so admirably, "the sensible appearance of the sensible, the silent persuasion of the sensible is Being's unique way of manifesting itself without becoming positivity, without ceasing to be ambiguous and transcendent."[25] Thus the sensible designates neither a constituent part nor a region of the world but the very element in which the world can appear, in which its irreducibility can be preserved. It is for this reason that talking of a *sensible world* is rooted in a tautology: there is a world only as a sensible world, but the sensible exists only as presentation of a world.

Perception and Living Movement

The critique of Husserl's subjectivism (and therefore of objectivism) has led to reformulation of the phenomenological reduction in order to elucidate the autonomy of appearance and describe its structure. The question of the "subject" of this appearance must now be returned to, inquiring into the sense of being of the person for whom there is a world and therefore a structure of horizon. Moreover, the description of appearance as such has already allowed one to glimpse the singular status of this subject. Far from constituting appearance, the subject is dependant on appearance; appearance of the subject to itself, the cogito as the test of my existence, refers to the general structure of appearance. By virtue of this structure, the experience of the self is necessarily, like any other manifestation, comanifestation of the world; the subject meets itself therefore only on the basis of a world and is consequently grounded in its relation to the latter. However, this cannot mean that the manifestation of the subject to whom the world appears can be identified with any manifestation. The subject does not appear as any being in the world from which I can step back but is given as the one *for* whom and *before* whom all this appears, as conditioning appearance at least in the negative sense in which its absence causes that of every manifestation.

In this regard, one cannot conceive of a manifestation that would not refer to a subject. The autonomy of appearance signifies that the world is not constituted by the subject, that the phenomenological given is the phenomenal field and not the lived experience; however, this does not imply that appearance can rely on itself and dispense with a subject. But neither must this subject be understood as an absolute sphere from which phenomenality would draw its meaning; it is an internal constitutive moment of phenomenality. The only absolute is phenomenality itself—"there is" something—and like the world the subject is relative. Its specificity derives from the fact that it polarizes the phenomenal field and thereby conditions appearance insofar as the latter is structured by the relationship between emptiness and fullness; in short, it comprises horizons. Thus the three constitutive moments of appearance mutually call each other forth. It is because appearance is necessarily appearance of a world (which does not appear in totality) that it is structured according to the polarity between actuality and horizon and that it is *consequently* appearance to someone. It is therefore for the same reason that the perceiving subject is the condition of the world and being in the world, phenomenalizing and finite; to the degree that the appearance of which it conditions always withdraws behind its manifestations, is given only in perspective, and under a certain aspect, the perceiving subject itself can only be situated being. The inscription of the perceiving subject in the world is the rigorous condition under which the perceiving subject can make the world appear as world.

Thus one is confronted with the heretofore unknown situation of a condition that can be conditioning only by being situated alongside that of which it is the condition, a transcendental that is delayed with respect to itself or that has always already preceded itself, such that it is necessarily enveloped by what it constitutes, inscribed in the empiricity it conditions. This is tantamount to saying that a subjective condition is only intraworldly, that the rooting in the empirical subject is itself a transcendental structure.[1] By virtue of the structure of belonging that describes the ultimate law of appearance, there is a subject of the world only if it is inscribed in the world, only if it is incarnated; "being face to face" with the world no longer forms an alternative to "being in its midst." It must be understood in the strict sense: the subjectivity of the subject requires its incarnation just as there is no body that is not a subject's body. The structure of appearance is therefore the actual questioning of the position, which goes back at least to Descartes, according to which the body is of a different order from that of thought or consciousness and can only constitute an obstacle to the latter's capacity for enlightenment. It is the sense of being of this subject, precisely insofar as it confuses the alternative between the psychic and the corporeal, that is now in question.

Moreover, it seems that, with regard to the clarification of this sense of being, Merleau-Ponty's approach is still not sufficiently radical. By relying on the Husserlian discovery of the constitution of the body itself in the sense of touch, he shows that the touching is tangible and that correlatively the body always envelops a sensibility, a conclusion that he generalizes by affirming that the seeing is visible by its nature. It is this analysis that allows him to disclose the implied subject in the world as inherent in the structure of appearance. Yet by proceeding in this way Merleau-Ponty remains dependent on a philosophy of consciousness insofar as such a philosophy relies upon the principle of an opposition between consciousness and body. Setting forth the confusion between touching and touched, he attempts to reduce the ontological distance between consciousness and body but does not challenge their duality; he finds in this confusion the ultimate phenomenon instead of understanding it as an invitation to search for a more profound sense of the being of the subject in which this distinction is rooted. From this is evident the difficulty with which one is left in analyzing flesh and chiasma. It is extraordinarily difficult to understand how touching can be touched, and inversely how my tangible body can prove to be sensible (such that it is apt to feel)—ultimately, how a sensibility can be immersed in a fragment of extension. In giving himself the body, Merleau-Ponty gives himself inevitably its difference from sensibility, and he then returns to the classic problem of union (as a species of the relation between touching and the tangible, seeing and the visible) instead of moving beyond it right away. Likewise, it is even more difficult to understand the mutual envelopment of subject and appearance so long as it is posed in terms of the body and flesh. Whether one wants to or not, the sensibility inherent in the body cannot be transferred as such to the flesh of the world, except by falling into a hylozoism that Merleau-Ponty himself rejects; the concept of flesh cannot be univocal once it is constructed on the basis of the body itself in which the distinction between extension and sensibility is ultimately preserved.

The reduction of the difference between the subject and the world by way of the flesh represents a kind of ontologization, indeed a kind of naturalization of a structure of manifestation in which its articulations are lost. The fact that the subject of appearance is inscribed in the world that appears through it does not mean that the subject and the world are two moments or aspects of one and the same carnal element. Subjectivity's mode of existing cannot be transferred as such to the world under the pretext that subjectivity is essentially incarnated; the fact that subjectivity envelops its own worldliness does not mean that worldliness itself envelops subjectivity. All that can be affirmed is that it envelops phenomenality—in short, that this world appears. Such is the starting point; this appearance also implies a worldly subject whose mode of existence must be questioned.

Certainly these difficulties did not escape Merleau-Ponty, but it is uncertain whether at the time he was writing *The Visible and the Invisible* he was in a position to resolve them. He objects, for example, that "the flesh of the world is not *self-sensing* [*se sentir*] as my flesh—It is sensible and not sentient—I call it flesh, nevertheless . . . in order to say that it is a *pregnancy* of possibles, *Weltmöglichkeit*."[2] Now, this is one of two things: either the concept of flesh is understood in the strict sense (but then assimilation would be unconceivable) or it names a mode of being that is none other than the radical immanence of sense with respect to facticity (but then the usage of the concept would seem unjustified, indeed misleading). An unpublished, undated note illustrates that such was in fact Merleau-Ponty's preoccupation:

Value of dualism—or rather refusal of an explanatory monism that would have recourse to an "intermediary" ontology. I am seeking an ontological middle ground, the field that will reunite object and consciousness. And it is imperative that we do so if we want to find our way out of idealist philosophy. However, the field, brute being (that of inanimate nature, that of the organism) must not be conceived of as a fabric from which object, consciousness, the order of causality and that of meaning would be cut.

Merleau-Ponty adds in the margin, in a significant way, "therefore, a radical clarification of the *esse-percipi* relationship is necessary"—which shows that he had yet to clarify this relationship fully. This is the crucial point because the risk represented precisely by "intermediary monism" is to subordinate the unity of the *esse* and the *percipi* to the *esse*, and to conceive of the appearance itself as an autonomous process in which the difference between modes of appearance would disappear, specifically between the body itself and the world. On the contrary, if we respect the unity of *esse* and *percipi*, if being and perceived being complement one another, we can no longer engulf the *percipere* in being by subordinating the body to the flesh; rather, one is led to preserve the phenomenal difference between object and consciousness and to question the specificity of the perceiving subject. Thus despite the change of level it implies, the shift from the *Phenomenology of Perception* to *The Visible and the Invisible* does not represent a decisive advance. The structure of phenomenality is approached starting from the specific phenomenon of the body itself, which appears from the beginning as the true transcendental. Moreover, even if this approach leads to a blurring of the encounter between the subject and the world and thus to revealing (beyond incarnation but due to it) the autonomy of appearance, it remains dependent on the inevitable characterization of the body as a unity, one that is certainly profound, of a sensibility and a materiality. Henceforth, the autonomy of appearance is interpreted in an ontologizing mode as an element replete with all meanings. This is why it is necessary to take as one's starting point the very structure of appearance and attempt to characterize the sense of the being proper to the subject (whose confusion between the felt and the feeling is only a manifestation) on the basis of this structure, instead of giving it to oneself immediately in the form of the body itself in order to deduce this structure from it after the fact, as Merleau-Ponty does.

If the subject is situated within the world, it exists in a mode entirely different from that of other worldly beings. As the mediator of appearance, it is adapted to its structure and exists in such a way that through it the presence of the unpresentability of the world within the horizon becomes possible. The fact that the subject cannot be conceived of as a sphere of immanence constituted by lived experiences does not mean that we must simply reduce it to the level of subject; on the contrary, its participation in appearance, which the theory of lived experience thematizes inadequately, refers to a mode of specific being. Moreover, as has been seen, the horizon is given as a certain nonbeing, or rather beyond the opposition between the positive and the negative, as the specific presence suitable to the irreducible absence of the world. The horizon is nothing more than this excess of any manifestation beyond itself, inherent in its constitutive belonging; in it the manifestation is given as the within or the negation of what cannot be otherwise positively exhibited.

It follows that the subject for which there is a world *necessarily involves a dimension of negativity.* To the excess of the manifestation beyond itself there cannot correspond a subject based on itself, existing in the mode of coincidence with itself, whatever the form of this coincidence. Only a subject that is its own excess or its own negation can correspond to the horizon, and in the latter it is situated at the antipodes of the thing that, by contrast, is characterized by its being based in itself and full of itself. To gain access to what creates the subjectivity of the subject, we must therefore not assume anything, but rather ask ourselves which worldly dimension (the corporeal) of perception manifests a radical eidetic difference with respect to other corporeal beings. Thus it is not sufficient to start from the fact that perception is incarnated, because the true question concerns the body's being insofar as it is what inscribes perception as such in the world, insofar as it is distinguished from the other material beings. The question therefore reads, What is the dimension of the body that is constitutive of perception and that on this basis must stand out against the mode of the being proper to the other material beings? What is the nature of the body insofar as it gives rise to a perception?

One has no choice but to concede that bodies that perceive are *living* bodies and that they are distinguished from other corporeal beings (moreover, but to a lesser degree, from the largely immobile living beings that are plants) by their capacity for *movement*. It is therefore on the level of this constitutive motility of the living being that we must be able to access the ultimate meaning of subjectivity; it is as subject capable of movement that the perceiving subject can be grasped in its true being. Hence, we point out that there is nothingness within the world only in the form of this concrete negativity to which a movement is reduced (which we must understand in the Aristotelian meaning of change). To move is not to be what one is (or was); it is to be always beyond and therefore within one's self, to exist on the basis of noncoincidence. *Within the "there is" there is negativity only as mobility*, because the latter represents the only negation that is not based on a positive nothingness and therefore does not compromise the fullness of this "there is." This interior negativity in the world must be taken as attesting to the constitutive negativity of the subject insofar as it is subject for the horizon. Thus it is possible to access the subjectivity within the world only on the basis of the concrete negativity of life. To determine the true being of the subject, it does not suffice therefore to grasp it as incarnated (which is tantamount to denying oneself the possibility of questioning the meaning of incarnation and to reactivating dualism). We must approach it instead on the basis of living movement, a constitutive characteristic of *its* incarnation.[3] What is more, to access the subject of appearance we must not approach its belonging as incarnation but as being-in-life; life is this mode of belonging in which a subjectivity as the condition of appearance can be attested. It follows, as will be seen later in this chapter, that instead of approaching life on the basis of the body, as the possibility characteristic of a body, we have to determine the body's sense of being based on life.

It is evident that in this regard we are subscribing to a particularly Aristotelian perspective. Far from considering the specificity of the vital as being exhausted in the presence of the psychic, whereby the remainder would be reduced to relations within extension, the "psychic" must be understood as a determination of the vital; being simply in life ("vegetative" soul), sensibility, and thought are moments of living being. Correlatively, perception is essentially linked to movement. Beings capable of moving are the very ones that are capable of feeling; feeling and moving are the two aspects of a same mode of living, because movement assumes the desire for a goal, which itself requires the capacity for perceiving it. Thus by inscribing perception in living being instead of dividing it according to the division between thought and extension, thereby showing the closeness of its relation to movement, Aristotle unquestionably opens the way toward a determination of the perceiving subject's specific mode of existing. The significance of our question concerning the subject's sense of being therefore becomes more precise in light of this evocation of living movement. If it is true that the subject of appearance is a living subject, therefore that there is a profound unity between its function of making appear and its being-in-life, one must conclude from this that *there is a sense of living that is deeper than the distinction between experiencing it (Erleben) and being-in-life (Leben).* The question of the sense of being proper to the subject insofar as it is indissolubly a condition of appearance and inscribed in the appearing world then merges with that of the question of this life that precedes the distinction between transitive living and intransitive living.

The difficulty in conceiving of the double condition of the subject stems from the fullness of the contrast between *res cogitans* and *res extensa* that leads us to conceive of perceptual experience only as transcending being in life and being in life only foreign to the perceptual order. On the contrary, if one succeeds in discovering a unitary sense of living that precedes, so to speak, the division of the characteristic and the metaphoric, one attains the subject's true sense of being according to the indissoluble unity between its being for the world and its being in the world. It is significant in this regard that, after having reduced the natural domain of the sciences and thus life in the sense of biology, Husserl describes the activity of transcendent subjectivity (which is effectuation of meaning) only in terms of life. This necessary metaphor clearly reveals something more profound than does the division between the characteristic and the metaphoric, a sense of life that precedes the division between the empiric and the transcendental. One realizes here "that the sole nucleus of the concept of *psyché* is life as self-relationship, whether or not it takes place in the form of consciousness. 'Living' is thus the name of that which precedes the reduction and finally escapes all the divisions which the latter gives rise to."[4]

We must still establish the constitutive relation between perception and movement beyond the empirical fact that living beings are the ones who perceive. This correlation has been established unquestionably by the important current of psychophysiological thought represented by Goldstein, who focuses in his research on the unitarian character of the organism in contrast with physiochemical or vitalist reductions. To take seriously the thesis of the irreducible character of organic totality is to recognize that what we call the somatic and the psychic are not constituent parts of the organism but expressions of organic totality, modalities of being in life. Hence sensibility and motility must be able to communicate since they involve two unquenstionable expressions of living being. Experience confirms this by what Goldstein calls the "tonic phenomena" that accompany especially optical and tactile impressions: "We can admit that for every sensory impression there corresponds a completely determined tension of musculature."[5] According to Goldstein, these tonic phenomena, which imply a certain type of movement, are part of the sensory phenomenon; insofar as it proceeds from a living subject, the sensibility of the senses involves the totality of the organism and therefore cannot be reduced to the grasp of a quality. This does not mean that sensation triggers a tonic phenomenon, nor that the muscular tension gives rise to a sensation, but rather that the sensation possesses a certain significance for the organism, a significance that is expressed also at the motor level. Movement on the one hand and the grasp of a determined quality on the other hand are two modalities by which the organism enters into a relation with a kind of event that makes sense for it. Beyond green as sensible content and more profoundly than it, there is the vital significance of green, the type of encounter that it represents for the organism, and this encounter is going to take indistinctly the form of movements of adduction and of the manifestation of a content. In other words, grasped from the point of view of the living being confronted there, the perceived necessarily possesses a dynamic significance; as the relation of an organic totality to an event in its midst, perception involves essentially an internal link with movement. This should be understood to mean that the act of perceiving consists in this tonic phenomenon by which the organism situates itself in relation to such an event, or rather that this act of presenting oneself in anticipation of the event gives rise to an irreducible mode of manifestation and therefore constitutes an originary form of perception.

It is this link between perception and movement that Von Weizsäcker places at the center of his research, which allows him to radicalize Goldstein's theses regarding the organism's unity and the totalizing nature of its relation with its milieu. This relation is conceived of in such a way that it escapes the alternative between physical causality and representative confrontation. Von Weizsäcker characterizes it as "encounter," thereby integrating a unitarian and dynamic relation: "Our examination has shown that the character of perception is neither organic nor inorganic, but that perception is in each instance a historic encounter between self and world, and that, involved with movement, it is always only a stage in the active evolution of this encounter towards an unknown goal."[6]

Hence perception and movement appear as two inextricably linked aspects of our relation with our surroundings, so that in certain cases, particularly with the perception of a movement, one can take on the role of the other. This is what he calls the "principle of equivalence": "In the motor system of bodily equilibrium, we can *replace* more or less completely a perception of movement by moving oneself, and . . . by contrast we can save ourselves an auto-movement by the perception of a movement."[7] Thus by grasping the relation of the living subject in its surroundings as a type of specific encounter possessing an immediately vital meaning, this psychophysiological approach succeeds in avoiding the alternative between the psychic and the corporeal and in elucidating the essential link between perception and movement. Strictly speaking, if perception is a certain relation between the living subject and its surroundings, movement forms part of its essence. In this context, the passage through the study of the living subject plays the role of a kind of phenomenological reduction in that it forces us to dispense with any positive psychic reality, whether representation or lived experience, and thus allows us to clarify the dynamism inherent in perception. If it is true that living subjects have an experience of what appears in their surroundings and enter into a relationship with an exteriority—even if they are entirely outside themselves and exist only in the dynamic mode, in short, if we cannot accord them reflective consciousness—we must conclude that movement is at the heart of perception. The move through psychophysiology therefore does not lead to a return to a primitive mode of existence but rather, owing to this suspension of any intellectual or reflective component, to a clarifying of an originary dimension of perceptual experience. When it involves the human person, this dimension is immediately concealed by the spontaneous introduction of the (all in all quite mysterious) concepts of lived experience, representation, or consciousness.

We must nevertheless arrive at the phenomenological level if we are to confirm what was established from the physiologist's external point of view and thus meet the objection that the movement toward perception in the strict sense (human perception) would coincide precisely with the disappearance of this motor relation, with the result that the perceiving subject ceases in this regard to be a living subject. Following Minkowski's line of reasoning, we can show first of all the presence of movement at the heart of perception by an analysis of attention. The latter must be defined as the act of "stopping there," as the delimitation of the object that, by chiseling out its contours, detaches it from its surroundings and enhances it. It is a *grasping*, comparable to the act by which I take an object in my hand; like manual grasping, attention draws near to the object and detaches it by delimiting its surface.[8] Attention is therefore an act that implies mobility. Doubly so, since first of all, as "stopping there," it is inscribed in an opposite movement of dispersion and separation; attention contrasts with the mobility of the object as with my own instability. But, it can compensate for this first mobility only by the firmness of its own movement. Second, attention is situated in continuity with perception (and with thought); it is conceived of as achieving what is already present in perception to the extent that we can speak of attentive and inattentive perception. If we conceive of perception therefore as an experience that is cut off from vital activity and consequently foreign to movement, if we understand it as the apprehension of an object that is already there and does not need the perceptual act to be delimited as such, then this continuity between attention and perception becomes incomprehensible. On the contrary, continuity can be reestablished only if we abandon this idea of perception and recognize that, since it is caught up in the dynamism of vital activity, it already implies an act of "stopping there"; it is an approach toward the object that grasps it beginning with its contours. As Minkowski points out: "If perception were only perception and thought nothing but thought and if they were not moreover, in regards to the dynamism of life, a stop there . . . we would not understand at all in what way, or better, by what 'mechanism,' attention is added to them in order to create something even more precise."[9] By virtue of its continuity with perception, attention as a gesture of grasping reveals its motor dimension; insofar as it is also a "stopping there," perception implies movement.

An attentive examination of visual or tactile perception confirms this. Fixation of an object implies a movement of the head and eyes, a movement that never ceases (the eyelids bat constantly) as if there were stability only if conquered by an instability.[10] Likewise, there is no tactile perception of an object without a movement of grasping, which involves the entire body such that the hand adopts in all its parts the position that allows it to conform to the exact contour of the object. As for the experience of superficial tactile qualities, it presupposes a displacement of the hand that is going to adopt speed appropriate for apprehension of bumpy, rough, or soft. Thus there is no perception without a movement that, so to speak, goes to meet the object, draws its contours, or adopts the angle that allows the clearest view of it. The mystery here is that, although preceding the perception of the object strictly speaking, movement is already adapted to it and "knows" the object before it is perceived. The hand would be unable to immediately conform to the complex form of an object or to communicate the required speed of movement so as to grasp the texture that it *is going* to perceive if the perception were not already prefigured in the movement, if the movement were not perceiving already in its own manner. As Merleau-Ponty points out in reference to vision: "We see only what we look at. What would vision be without eye movement? And how could the movement of the eyes bring things together if the movement were blind? If it were only reflex? If it did not have its antennae, its clairvoyance? If vision were not prefigured in it?"[11]

We must therefore recognize that movement itself refers to the object on the basis of a mode that is irreducible to an objective and mechanical displacement; it is familiar with the object—there is a perception within movement. It does not involve a perception distinct from it that would guide it or subsist in it in an implicit or unconscious way. Such an interpretation is rooted in an inability to conceive of experience other than on the basis of psychic contents, foreign to the order of exteriority (in other words, in an inability to recognize the autonomy of appearance). In truth, it is *movement itself* that perceives in the sense that the object exists *for* it, in which movement has its meaning, as its oriented nature attests, inspired and clairvoyant with regard to the living movement that often demonstrates an intimacy with its objective, an intimacy that runs deeper than that which knowledge exhibits. In and by movement the object appears, though without its manifestation being separated from its brute presence, according to the indistinctness between its essence and its existence. Here the grasp of the object is not distinguished from the gesture made toward it; perception takes place in the world and not in me, and the object is therefore perceived where it is. We are confronted by a strictly motor perception that unfolds exclusively in exteriority and rejoins rather than represents the object. Patočka speaks of a "seeing force" that "must contain something like a clarity, a light by means of which it illuminates its way by itself."[12]

Certainly the movement in which perception takes place has a specific status, one that distinguishes it from an objective displacement; it is what justifies our talk of automovement or "subjective" movement. The corporeality of perception has as its opposite the "subjectivity" of the corporeal movement. However, we must understand the usage of this term—which serves to distinguish my movement from the spatial displacement of any object—as the indication of a problem. My movement is precisely never the external effect of a subjectivity that would be independent of it and would possess itself, so that the discovery of this movement is an invitation to redefine subjectivity. My movement is by no means the effectuation in space of an immanent decision; the decision is not distinguished from its implementation, the subjective impulse from its objective exteriorization. Subjective movement is characterized by the fact that the intention is its own fulfillment; the aim is its own realization, or rather, the movement appears as the actual opposition of these distinctions. It is this potency that has no reality outside its implementation, an "I can" that exists only as an "I am doing." Thus a singular type of adequacy is realized by means of the lived movement: when the experience becomes one with movement, one with its realization, the movement cannot be lived as other than what it is. Movement is the realized identity between being and appearance. This leads us to affirm that, as soon as this identity of being and appearance is achieved, all modalities of certitude must involve a motor dimension. As Patočka suggests, "Perhaps the reflection's certitude of self stems from the fact that it involves a particular kind of internal movement."[13] Far from being the negation of immanence, movement would be its condition of realization. Whatever the case, we are dealing here with a singular type of subjectivity that is its own passage in exteriority and whose immanence is realized only by a leap into transcendence. The subject exists only on the basis of its own withdrawal; it is fulfilled only by being exteriorized. It is the effective identity between an ipseity and an ecstasy, and if one can still call it a subject, it is in the sense of a being that is its own quest and that therefore possesses its essence outside itself.

However, here it must be added that by becoming movement the impulse is not lost in exteriority; rather the realization of the "I" in movement involves just as much the restraint of movement within pure exteriority—in other words, within an objective displacement in which movement is nothing but its effective unfolding. Conceiving of the realization as an objective displacement would be tantamount to restoring the position of a consciousness fundamentally foreign to exteriority. Consequently, the subject can exceed itself only because this movement remains within a simple objective journey; the exteriorization of the subject in movement has as its counterpoint the ebb of movement toward a form of interiority. Lived movement has the characteristic that the power from whence it proceeds is not exhausted but on the contrary is reactivated by its implementation. Living movement is automovement not only because it proceeds from the self but above all because it is its own source, because it nourishes itself, and because the impulse is not exhausted but restored by its realization.

The true meaning of the subject consists in this autonomy of living movement, this capacity for continually recreating one's self. The subject is not that which, at the source of movement, would find itself always restored by what dispossesses it; rather, it corresponds to this tension typical of living movement, which is manifest in the fact that it remains always withdrawn from itself, such that no realization fulfills it; its subjectivity is merged with the irreducible excess of its potency over its acts. In other words, instead of referring the impulse to a subject that would then be exterior to the movement, it is necessary to understand that the subject is nothing but the impulse itself as the excess of movement beyond its accomplishments, a dynamic reserve. There is a subject of movement only as the subject *in* movement, insofar as it is born of its internal excess.[14] Living movement has the peculiar quality that it always summons resumption, such that immobility is always only a pause in this instance, a suspension and therefore a modality of movement, as if in each finished movement were affirmed another movement for which the former is still only immobility. If there is an "I can" only on the basis of an "I am doing," it is just as true to say that there is an "I am doing" only as an "I can," that each living movement is not so much the realization as the restoration of an exigency (as if it were able to remain only on this side of what it focuses upon) and that any implementation is the affirmation of a potency that exceeds it. Thus the subject of movement is nothing more than the ensemble of its actualizations while nevertheless not merging with them.

The excess of capacity beyond action does not mean that ability can exist other than as action and therefore does not contradict their identity; even though all action assumes an ability, there is ability only as action. Hence the fact that the lived experience of movement merges with its effectuation does not exclude the emergence in this lived movement of a dimension that exceeds all effectuation; the fact that the subject coincides with the effectiveness of movement, since there is energy only as achievement, does not mean that the subject is identified with movement and therefore does not prevent it from involving a dimension that transcends effectiveness. The living subject is nothing more than this unassignable excess beyond any final position that is not sustained by any positivity and is therefore identified just as much with each of these positions. The subject merges with the negativity typical of living movement, with this distance —simultaneously unassignable and insurmountable—that separates movement from itself, its energy from its effectuations, and whence proceeds its dynamic. Movement is therefore both penetration into exteriority and the ability for indefinite renewal; it rejoins the thing where it is, but it cannot stop there, because any location calls for a new fulfillment. It is exploration in the sense that, as the most cursory observation of animal behavior shows, its only aim is to gain what can nourish its quest, each pause being satisfying and providing rest only to the degree that it gives new impetus to the movement of exploration.

Movement thus defined conjoins the two constitutive characteristics of perception. Movement attains the thing itself because it is an entry into exteriority; however, insofar as it is also an ability for renewal, it attains it only as what gives impetus to a new movement, as what none of these encounters can exhaust. What appeared therefore to be irreconcilable from the point of view of a philosophy of consciousness becomes perfectly coherent once we understand perception starting with motility. It is for the same reason that living movement rejoins the object itself and that no object exhausts it, that movement makes the object appear and indefinitely repels its manifestation; because it is not a simple mechanical displacement subject to the principle of inertia, its capacity for penetrating reality in order to attain the thing itself does not function without an opposite capacity for placing at a distance and for surpassing. Rather, this entry into exteriority depends on a restless energy that leads at the same time to the surpassing of any finished position.

There is a kind of volubility or inconstancy proper to living movement that causes it to be able to attain an effective position only on the condition of abandoning it, to have a goal destined only to become a future beginning. The excess beyond the self that could serve to define movement and that allows it to obtain the thing itself is such that it always exceeds itself, transforms itself out of this excess, and therefore calls forth a new movement; this is why perception attains the thing itself, although the latter is never given itself. One could say that the givenness of the thing corresponds to the effectuation of movement, and that its withdrawal in this givenness corresponds to the infinite excess of ability beyond action. However, this would be an abstract description because movement is precisely the unity of ability and its realizations.

In any event, because this active transcendence typical of movement exists to some extent only on the level of the second power and therefore always transcends itself, there is exterior existence only involving a new depth, the thing present in the flesh only requiring new determinations and proximity only calling for a new approach. The "movement" of adumbrating that required the difficult conciliation between revealing and concealing is understood starting from the differentiated unity between ability and action that characterizes living movement. One could therefore say, following Merleau-Ponty (who in no other work goes as far regarding this question as in his lecture course on nature) that movement is to perception what inquiry is to response.[15] If one understands inquiry rigorously, not as the factual absence of an answer that could terminate it but as dissatisfaction that is reactivated by the objects upon which it bears, then living movement has much in common with an inquiry: it regains the object only in order to extract from it what it needs in order to give new impetus to its dynamism, and the former is given only as what exhibits a depth that attracts exploration. The perceived is therefore nothing more than what, within appearance, within this originary appearing that is the world, is attained by movement as that which calls forth an indefinite continuation of this movement, specifically as horizon. To recognize that the perceived is presented as a horizon is to understand that it can be rejoined only by a movement that is its own excess and therefore that it can be grasped only as what must still be approached. The "horizon(t)al" structure of appearance and the inscription of perception in a living movement are the two sides of an identical situation; the nonpositive excess of the horizon over any manifestation responds to the unassignable difference of ability over action.

It is in this sense that we understand a note from the aforementioned lecture course on nature, which is, in our view, the most radical thing Merleau-Ponty wrote regarding perception:

Do not conceive of esthesiology as descent from a thought into a body. This is tantamount to renouncing esthesiology. Do not introduce a "to perceive" without corporeal "links." No perception without prospective movements, and consciousness of moving is not thought of an objective change of place, we do not move as a thing, but by a reduction of separation, and perception is merely the other pole of this separation, the maintained separation.[16]

Merleau-Ponty acknowledges that the corporeal inscription of perceiving, the intraworldliness of the perceiving subject, consists in a prospective movement. On the other hand, by introducing the concept of separation he recognizes the interrogative dimension of movement and therefore the originary unity of perception and movement. In contrast to objective movement, living movement unfolds from a term that polarizes it from the outset.

It is not a blind surpassing of each attained position but the reduction of a separation; it is not distance traveled but accomplishment. The manifestation of the perceived is what simultaneously fills and hollows out the separation, such that each completed perception calls forth other prospective movements. Thus perception and movement appear as two sides or dimensions of the same fundamental event. Movement is an attempt at reducing a separation. However, by virtue of its fundamental tension of the constitutive excess of ability beyond action, the separation is maintained, which is why movement gives rise to a perception. Perception therefore appears as the opposite of movement's nonfulfillment. Inversely, it is because the separation is maintained in perception that the latter gives new impetus to movement, calls for new exploration; it is because no perception can calm movement's constitutive tension that it gives rise to new perceptions. In this sense, movement is the other side of perception's nonfulfillment. Perception and movement appear, so to speak, as the two poles of the same separation; because reduction occurs only on the basis of a separation, movement refers to perception, but because separation is effected only when reduced being is sought, perception refers to movement.

Of course, the difficulty is to understand which separation is involved here. What is this distance that movement tries to reduce and that is given in the form of perception? What is the nature of this unity that is aimed at by movement and whose fold is given as a perceived reality? What is presented at such a distance that movement can reduce it only partially by giving rise to circumscribed perceptions? The response to these questions demands a thorough analysis of the nature of movement and therefore of living.

One sees that the reinterpretation of perception is connected with a redefinition of movement, or rather that an authentic determination of perception is possible only as a characterization of living movement. Moreover, on further consideration, this recognition of an intimacy between perception and movement involves nothing incomprehensible once we cease to understand appearance as the presentation of an object and consequently manifestation as subordinated to a consciousness. By virtue of the autonomy of appearance, the role of perception cannot be to produce the manifestation but to actualize it, to wrest it from the background of the world in which it is inscribed. This is why perception is essentially mobility once the movement of drawing nearer or of exploring, as just described, respects the phenomenal field's autonomy even while bringing it to actuality. If it is true that perception is preceded by the intrinsic perceptibility of the world, that *esse est percipi*, its proper work can consist only in actualizing this perceptibility; this is why it is realized as movement. By grasping perceiving subjectivity through living movement, one rigorously reconciles the subject's belonging to the world with its power of revealing, inherent in its status of condition of manifestation. Thus perceptual manifestation ultimately arises from the strict relation between a movement and a phenomenal field, and it is by no means necessary to introduce any psychic reality whatsoever; the properly active moment of perception in which the autonomy of a subjectivity is confirmed resides in motility, which is why perception as such is indifferent to the division between the psychic and the corporeal.

By affirming the autonomy of appearance in relation to any subjective positivity and therefore by reducing the subject's function in perception to its motor activity, we align ourselves closely with the thesis developed by Bergson in chapter 1 of *Matter and Memory*. By refusing to interiorize reality in the subject, as well as to posit a reality foreign to perceptual experience, Bergson introduces the concept of *image* in order to characterize the sense of being of the real. By the latter he understands a reality that is situated midway between the spatiotemporal object and the idea; it is unquestionable both that the real is nothing more than what appears to us (the idea of a reality in itself that would be situated behind what we perceive is incomprehensible) and that what appears to us is real (it is just as unacceptable to affirm that what we perceive is in us and not a reality outside us). In short, the concept of image is the exact expression of an identity between the *esse* and the *percipi*.

The approach to perception is singularly transformed by this fact. First of all (and this is extremely important), one must abandon the idea that perception could depend on a psychic reality born of the brain, and that the brain could produce a representation of the universe. The brain is only one image among other images; it is included within the totality of images and therefore cannot itself understand the totality. As the homogeneity of the medulla oblongata and the cerebral tissue confirms, the brain can produce movement only as does the spinal cord. For Bergson, it is therefore a question of accounting for perception without introducing something like a representation, without abandoning the univocal level of images. One must account for the difference between being and perceived being on the level of images only, hence without involving any psychic dimension, which by definition is foreign to images. As was suggested earlier, this is tantamount to accounting for perception on the basis of a subject that is situated within the appearing, on the basis of a living being. Bergson's solution consists in thematizing the difference between being and perceived being only on the level of images, starting with the difference between two types of movement.

It must be said here that images in general are governed by the laws of nature; they are satisfied with receiving impulses and transmitting them mechanically. More precisely, each image is only a place through which passes the energy emerging from all the others, something like a "world crossroads" such that, strictly speaking, it passes itself in the other images or is not distinguished from the totality of which it is a part. Each image is merely its transitive relation with all the others; it cannot be distinguished from the others because nothing occurs to stop the flows that travel through it. This is why what exists "before" perception is not *images* but only the whole of the images, from which not a single one is detached. Moreover, the living body (cerebralized) is distinguished from other images insofar as it is capable of stopping the impulse coming from them, from the exterior world; with the living subject emerges another type of movement, and it is starting with this movement that we account for perception.

Because the brain divides the impulse coming from the outside via a multitude of cerebral paths so that reaction is delayed, the living subject can circumscribe an image within the totality of images. Instead of traveling through the body, as would happen with another image, the impulse from the outside comes to be reflected on this center of resistance that is the brain and thus to draw the contours of the object from which it emanates. In the case of a simple organism, perception of the outside object's action merges with the reaction it provokes; the immediacy of the reaction goes hand-in-hand with the absence of perception. Moreover, if an immediate reaction corresponds to an absence of perception, *it can be inferred that perception originates in the reaction's delay.* A more complex organism perceives to the exact degree to which the reaction does not immediately follow the stimulus, to the degree to which it can be delayed. Thus, as Bergson writes, *"perception is the master of space to the exact degree to which action is the master of time."*[17]

By reacting in a way that is no longer mechanical to the stimuli of the outside world, the living subject circumscribes within this exteriority the aspects that have a vital meaning. The distance that characterizes the perceived object is only the expression of the temporal delay of the reaction that it is going to provoke. Perception therefore originates in the distance that separates the external impulse from the reaction; the image that remains invisible as long as its action travels through the body without meeting resistance sees its action stopped by the living body insofar as it selects and delays the adapted reaction; by ceasing to be lost in its other, it thereby becomes circumscribed as an object. According to the comparison proposed by Bergson, everything happens as if shining rays outlined the contours of the object that emits them by being reflected on an opaque screen. Hence there is an exact correspondence between the extension of what is perceived and the sphere of needs (and aversions): what is perceived is only that which the living subject reacts to, and the living subject reacts only to that which possesses a vital significance (prey, threat, and so on). Vital activity sketches the world, the environment that corresponds to it. To say that perception relies on a certain type of movement, namely living movements, characterized by the adaptation of the reaction, is to recognize that the field of the perceived does not exceed the field of what is vitally significant.

One should not, however, conclude hastily from this that the possibility of accounting for the sphere of objects strictly speaking, and thus for a thematic relation with the world, is compromised because in Bergson's view circumscribing a universe of objects is precisely the characteristic typical of vital action, and in the case of the human person the characteristic of creative activity. The object is not born of a disinterested relation to the world; it is on the contrary constituted by vital activity and, more generally, by action that needs to circumscribe stable entities within a flowing totality. Far from representing a rupture vis-à-vis the order of vital action, language and intelligence are only extensions of it, elevating its discriminating power a little higher. Hence, a disinterested relation to the world does not result in the emergence of an objective order; rather, it leads to its dissolution. It is intuition.

Nevertheless, if it is true that perception originates from vital action, which carves out what interests it in responding to certain external stimuli in an adapted way, the fact that we are concerned with a *conscious* perception still remains to be accounted for (the fact that the presence of the circumscribed object stems from a *representation*). Moreover, to pose this question is to forget that the living subject's action takes place within a universe of images, of realities that do not exist outside their relation to a possible consciousness and therefore are legitimately perceptible. The problem of the passage from the presence of images to their representation is thus posed in terms opposite those of the traditional approach:

If, in order to pass from presence to representation, it were necessary to add something, the barrier would indeed be insuperable, and the passage from matter to perception would remain wrapt in impenetrable mystery. It would not be the same if it were possible to pass from the first term to the second by way of diminution, and if the representation of an image were *less* than its presence; for it would then suffice that the images present should be compelled to abandon something of themselves in order that their mere presence should convert them into representations.[18]

Moreover, this is precisely what happens with the body's action. By circumscribing the image and delimiting certain aspects of it, the body's action detaches the image from the totality and therefore transforms it into representation. All images are legitimately perceptible, and it is their insertion in nature, the fact that nothing stops their action and that they are therefore lost in the whole, that explains why they are not in fact perceived. Perception, the passage of the thing to its manifestation, corresponds strictly to the possibility of circumscribing the image within the totality; *perceiving* an image is perceiving *an* image. Consciousness refers to representation that must itself be included in the strict sense of a "putting into a picture." Through an encounter with a living body that detaches from it what responds to its vital needs, the image loses most of its relations to the totality and thereby becomes its own surface (what Bergson calls the "envelope"); it is rigorously from this putting into representation that a representation is born in the sense of a conscious manifestation. Although the existence in itself of the image corresponds to the ensemble of the relations it maintains with the totality, its existence for itself signifies the rupture between these relations and the circumscription of its own identity. Paradoxically, to say that the image is for me is to say that it is itself, that it is distinguished from the totality. It follows, as Bergson points out, that I perceive the object itself and not some double or "representation" thereof; this is the case because I perceive it in itself, where it is.

We see that Bergson succeeds in accounting for the difference between the thing and its perception on the basis of just the difference between two types of movement within the ontologically homogeneous sphere of images, without ever introducing something like a psychic or intellectual reality that would bear precisely the burden of representation. His analysis is therefore determined by two fundamental decisions that mutually require each other. On the one hand, phenomenality does not need to be based on a specific level because it is constitutive of being itself. Any reality refers essentially to a possible perception; the *esse* refers to a *percipi* that is not underpinned by a *percipere*. On the other hand, perception strictly speaking that accounts for the difference between a thing and its manifestation consists in a movement and consequently is rooted in the living being. Contrary to what traditional philosophy affirms, perception has in no way a speculative interest; it is not knowledge but *action*. It is clear that by allowing himself the autonomy of the phenomenal field Bergson suspends the question regarding the source of appearance and thus avoids positing the existence of any psychic reality whatsoever. Perception is the fact of an intraworldly being, an image, and its specificity can be only in its mode of movement—the perceiving subject is a living subject. It is the singularity of this movement explaining the emergence of specific manifestations that accounts for perception. Thus, as was suggested earlier, perceptual manifestation does indeed proceed in this instance from the strict relation between living movement and phenomenal field, which is why the eternal question of the relation of perceptual representation to its object is immediately resolved. Insofar as it stems from movement, perception is satisfied with focusing on the thing itself in order to circumscribe it; it is intentional because of its motility. The first chapter of *Matter and Memory* therefore establishes for the first time what seem to be the conditions of a rigorous theory of perception.

However, we must admit that this leaves us feeling uneasy. Bergson defines reality as an ensemble of images by virtue of the undeniable fact that, if the real is correlative to our experience, the latter is nevertheless experience of the real.[19] Thus being is identical to perceived being because perceived being truly is. Yet how can one conceive of this perceived being without a subject that conditions it? As was seen earlier, recognizing the autonomy of appearance cannot lead us to dispensing with a subjective pole conditioning this appearance, with a singular being to whom all this appears. For Bergson, this pole merges with the living subject that circumscribes a definite image within the totality of images that is strictly perceived. Now, as Bergson himself recognizes, vital action can determine the passage from presence to representation because representation is preceded in presence insofar as the latter is part of the totality of images. This means that even if the totality of images is not strictly speaking an image, the manifestation of images in the strict sense is possible only because this totality is already appearing. Thus there are two options: either vital action can account by itself for perception (this would mean that the totality from which the image is detached is already appearance and *consequently requires a specific subject*) or we ignore this situation (but then the emergence of perception within the totality would become purely and simply incomprehensible). The constitution of perception based on a simple selection, on a negation, is conceivable only within a being that is already perceptibility and that by virtue of this refers already to a perceiving subject. In other words, if the perception of an object is preceded within the totality of images, the subject of this perception must also be preceded in the form of a subject *for this totality.*

The true difficulty does not lie therefore in understanding how perception emerges against a background of the totality of images, but in grasping how this totality can be totality *of images,* how it can already contain their perceived being and consequently how this perception can be at the same time a relationship to the totality. Moreover, it must be admitted that the correlative subject of the appearance of totality is absent from Bergson's description. There is nothing in the cerebralized living subject that can account for totality, for the presupposed appearance by perceptual activity. Its very activity does not involve any phenomenalizing or intentional dimension; it is reduced to an ensemble of reactions according to vital necessities. The totality of images cannot refer to a particular subject and therefore is not itself an image, such that the perceptual activity referred to the living subject's activity presupposes appearance instead of truly accounting for it. One could just as well say that by refusing to conceive of the possibility of the image on the level of totality, Bergson appropriates appearance in the form of a preliminary reality and thus relapses into a subtler form of realism. Because it is not supported by a determination of the corresponding subjective pole, the identity of the *esse* and the *percipi* is ultimately subordinated to the primacy of the *esse*. This is undoubtedly what Merleau-Ponty means when he writes, in lecture notes regarding Bergson: "Bergson deduces the perceived from being rather than admitting, as he had been tempted to do, a primacy of perception, a kind of intermediate existence between the In Itself and the For Itself. He does not really look for the starting point of the subject's knowledge of being in the subject's situation in being, but places himself directly in being in order to then introduce the perceptual découpage."[20]

Thus the degradation of the *percipi* to *esse*, of appearance to a real totality, has for its correlative a perceiving subject that does not possess any phenomenalizing power, that is reduced to its vital activity and is satisfied with choosing within the totality. But what then remains incomprehensible is that this carving out can give rise to a manifestation, that phenomenal can be born of this play between movements. In this regard, even if this observation occurs in a critical context with which we do not agree, Merleau-Ponty is undoubtedly not wrong when he says, "There is in Bergson, then, a blindness toward the proper being of consciousness and its intentional structure."[21] The blind spot in Bergson's creation is therefore the properly subjective dimension that would account within the living subject for appearance against a background from which the singular image can be detached. Bergson subjugates his conception of the perceiving subject to a preliminary idea of the living subject instead of rethinking the sense of being proper to the living subject in light of perceptual activity.

Nevertheless, it should be added that what we interpret as a failure from the phenomenological point of view makes perfect sense from the perspective of Bergson's undertaking. The description from the first chapter of *Matter and Memory* concerns what he calls "pure perception," perception as it would take place instantaneously. One could say that this perception depends on an abstraction: effective perception is inscribed in duration, and the instant (however brief we imagine it) involves a lapse of time. It is this inscription in duration, insofar as it allows the intervention of memory, that accounts for the properly subjective dimension of perception, a dimension that is understood ultimately in rather a classic way as the *recognition* of what is given in the actuality of the action. Recognition is defined as the act by which recollections involve a current perception, and the difficulty is understanding how recollections that are of a purely spiritual order can coincide with the only thing of which the brain is capable: movements.

Thus the duality between the psychic and the corporeal that was set aside in the name of the ontological univocity of images and the homogeneity of nerve tissues is not rescued but *displaced* in a form that is radicalized as a duality between memory and matter. The realism that we criticized on the level of the theory of images thus appears as the counterpart of a spiritualism; the moment of the cogito, the subjective character of perceptual life is transferred to a positive spiritual reality, and the description of pure perception (by being situated on the strict cerebral and motor level) lays the groundwork for recourse to memory as the unique means of accounting for the totality of the perceptual phenomenon.

Yet in this formulation, which is based on a duality that is of a metaphysical nature, the essential is lost. By determining perception to be movement, Bergson does not focus on grasping perception at the very level of living movement in order to elucidate a renewed sense of the subject. On the contrary, he focuses on preparing the articulation with a dimension fundamentally foreign to matter, a dimension in which the being of subjectivity ultimately resides. As Merleau-Ponty states clearly: "The body does not succeed in being a subject—though Bergson tends to give it this status—for if the body were subject, the subject would be body, and this is something Bergson does not want at any price."[22]

One is therefore led to reevaluate the significance of the theory of images. It aims at describing the reality that is correlative of vital action, and at revealing the dependence of perception (as separation and objectivation) on the very exigencies of life; it in no way claims to establish the identity of being and phenomenality. In truth, the description of reality as an ensemble of images is provisional and constitutes a basis of a deeper elaboration. Since it is not an image, the whole of images must be defined in itself, independently of any reference to a living subject; such is the stake of the metaphysical analysis of matter that is the focus of chapter 4 of *Matter and Memory* and that is taken up again in *Creative Evolution*.

However, if the limits of the theory of perception from Chapter 1 of *Matter and Memory* are understood from the point of view of the specificity of Bergson's undertaking, they are extremely illuminating in that they allow us to characterize more precisely the conditions to which a theory of perception is subjected, a theory that grasps the perceptual subject through the living subject. If we abandon the idea of a subjectivity that would attain the object on the basis of lived experiences; if we contrast it with a perception that, in proceeding from a living subject, merges with movement, then the study of chapter 1 of *Matter and Memory* teaches us that this assimilation of perceptual movement by vital movement must be accompanied by precise reservations; in this regard it would be fair to say that our perspective is situated between Husserl and Bergson. We have seen that assimilation of perception by movement proceeds from recognition of the autonomy of appearance as an appearance of the world and therefore of the intraworldly character of the perceiving subject.

As Bergson has shown, the role of perception can be only to actualize an intrinsic perceptibility, to lead appearance to effective manifestation. This actualization can consist only in a negation, in circumscribing a perceived object against the background of a preliminary totality. Any manifestation is a comanifestation of the world; any appearing is detached from an untotalizable totality in which it is inscribed. However, if Bergson recognizes this negative dimension of perception inherent in its motor constitution, he does not account for the preliminary totality whose originary manifestation allows singular manifestations, so that he appropriates phenomenality instead of understanding its possibility derived from the subject. Moreover, the manifestation of the world is part of the structure of appearance; there is a singular manifestation only as a comanifestation of a world. The perceiving subject that circumscribes the singular manifestation must therefore be simultaneously the *subject for the totality* of which this manifestation is the negation. This is the aspect that Bergson does not succeed in accounting for because, if the living subject is indeed the condition for the singular image, it is inscribed in the totality of images without conditioning its dimension of image, its phenomenality. Yet it is clear that it is the same subject that circumscribes the manifestation as the negation of the totality and that carries the possibility of the totality of which it is the negation.

One cannot reintroduce in the subject a specific dimension by which it would relate to the totality as such, an ability to dominate the world and to determine it adequately—in short, something like a thought; on the contrary, it is with regard to such an approach (which is still Husserl's) that Bergson's analysis demonstrates its value. Insofar as it is all-encompassing, the world is essentially what can be neither dominated nor adequately given, which is why it disappears from everything that manifests it. The negative character of manifestations is the correlative of the unpresentability of the world. It is therefore through living movement that we must grasp in a unitary way the possibility of the manifestation and that of the comanifestation of the world it negates; we can account for perception that is based on movement only on the condition of elucidating a sense of being proper to the motor subject in which are constituted conjointly the manifestation and the totality of which the manifestation is the negation. Moreover, to the degree that, as motor, the subject can circumscribe its object only within the phenomenal field and to the degree that the manifestation of the phenomenal totality as such cannot rely on a nonvital (extraworldly) dimension, we must conclude from this that the movement from which perception proceeds constitutes totality in the act by which it negates it and therefore that there is a positing of totality only as its own negation. We are not asserting here the view that totality is given only in forms in which it is negated, but rather that it is in its negation that the totality as such is posited, as if the part were to give rise to the whole of which it is a part. The perceiving subject is defined by the fact that the movement it unfolds opens onto the totality in the very act by which it negates it by determining it in the form of a concrete manifestation. We find ourselves here midway between Husserl's and Bergson's positions: if perception is indeed a condition of the world, this conditionality cannot be based on an autonomous psychic order, and it must therefore proceed from vital activity itself, so that it is indeed in movement itself that the world must be constituted, a world that movement considers as the field against the background of which its negating power unfolds.

    In truth, this conclusion arises from a rigorous consideration of the problem's conditions. The subject can be a condition of appearance, and therefore a subject for the world, while being an intraworldly subject only if the movement that it deploys within the world is simultaneously a movement that opens up the world, only if its movement *in* the world is simultaneously movement *toward* the world—only if it unfolds the totality according to its finite negations. Moreover, it has been seen that Bergson's inability to conceive of the subject as the subject of the totality of images had as a counterpart his characterization of life as a reaction to external stimuli according to need. It is because the totality is pregiven in a realistic mode that the living subject is reduced to the minimalist sense of vitality as the satisfaction of needs. By the same token, it is because Bergson can conceive of vital subjectivity, the difference between vital movement vis-à-vis mechanical movement, only in terms of need that he cannot account for totality with respect to its subjective pole and thus justify the identity between being and appearance at the level of totality. It follows that living movement, and therefore the perceptual subject's sense of being that we are attempting to circumscribe, must be sought *beyond the dimension of strict need*. If need can circumscribe a presence, it cannot transcend it toward the whole of which it is the negation; the manifestation of the object that satisfies it is the negation and never the positing of totality. Thus the subject's sense of being we are seeking is indeed situated at a midway point between need (which rejoins its object only at the cost of the negation of totality) and thought (which rejoins the totality only at the cost of a negation of the singular presence). The subject of perception exists in a mode such that it has access to totality only in and by the finite presence that negates it.

5

Desire as the Essence of Subjectivity

It has been shown that the perceptual act, which is not the constitution but the co-condition of appearance, must be conceived of as a motor act; it therefore refers to the specificity of living movement. This corresponds to the intraworldly dimension of the perceiving subject insofar as it is at the same time the conditioning pole of appearance. It now remains to characterize the very being of the perceiving subject whose perceptual activity has been shown to merge with these specific movements, and consequently to inquire into the essence of the living subject. To what more originary dimension do the living moments that give rise to perception refer? How must we define the unitary subject that is affirmed in each of these movements? Patočka approaches the problem this way: "The question arises to know whether subjective movements are to be conceived of as a multiplicity of particular acts, or whether we could not legitimately see in them the modalities of a fundamental global movement that would coincide with living itself as far as it unfolds towards the outside."[1]

This inquiry provides two valuable insights. First of all, subjectivity itself must be conceived of as a movement, so that from movement as objective displacement and living automovement we must distinguish a third kind of movement, one that is the condition of the preceding one and therefore the condition for spatialization rather than being strictly spatial, as is living movement. Second, this movement must coincide "with living itself insofar as it unfolds towards the outside", which is tantamount to saying that living movement refers to the movement of life itself and therefore forces us to attempt to characterize the dynamic at the heart of vital existence.

To do this we must return to our point of departure: how Husserl approaches perception. This is characterized as an intuition, as an act that fulfills empty intentionality by confronting the thing itself in person that consequently satisfies the need for fulfillment inherent in merely signitive intentionality. As has been seen, empty intentionality is already a relationship with the object itself, though in a mode of absence; the relation of signitive intentionality to the intuitive act possesses a dynamic signification that expresses the teleological orientation of consciousness toward knowledge, toward full presence. Therefore the absence of the object is incompleteness; empty intentionality is a need for fullness (a tension), and intuitive presence is satisfaction. This affective aspect, so to speak, of the description of intentionality appears clearly in a number of texts prior to the *Logical Investigations* in which precisely this division of acts is elaborated.[2] In them Husserl points out that intentional consciousness, in the form of empty intentionality, engenders a *Gemütsaffekt* of consciousness that consists in a feeling of dissatisfaction. The intentional dynamic that leads consciousness toward an intuitive presentation of the object is rooted in a tension (*Spannung*) that is inherent in this dissatisfaction; in keeping with the tendency toward knowledge, consciousness seeks to annul the tension, which is why the object's intuitive presence is experienced as satisfaction. In the description, the intervention of an affective component that contrasts with the objectivating movement it qualifies contains nothing surprising; the movement toward fullness, the tendency not to hold to the purely signitive presence, is comprehensible only if the object's absence is experienced as incompleteness, as creating a tension. Thus because he conceives of intentionality as originarily oriented toward the object, Husserl describes it as aiming at a presentation, as a movement toward fullness. However, because of this very dynamic, he must introduce into it a dimension that exceeds its objectivating significance: that of tendency. As Lévinas points out:

Husserl himself imperceptively introduces into his description of intention an element that is different from pure thematization: intuition fills (that is, contents or satisfies) or deceives an aim aiming emptily at its object. From the emptiness that a symbol involves with respect to the image which illustrates the symbolized, one passes to the emptiness of hunger. Here there is a *desire* outside of the *simple consciousness* of. . . . It is still an intention, but intention in a sense radically different from theoretical aim, and the practice that theory involves. Intention is now taken as desire, such that intention, occurring between deception and *Erfüllung*, already reduces the "objectifying act" to a specification of a tendency, rather than hunger being a particular case of "consciousness of."[3]

By describing objectivating intentionality as the fulfillment of empty intentionality, Husserl therefore introduces into it a determination that paradoxically calls into question the primacy of objectivating acts. If the dynamic of presentation characterizing intentionality can be understood only on the basis of a tendency rooted in a tension and aimed at satisfaction, one must conclude that at the heart of objectivation there is a deeper movement that defines the originary meaning of intentionality. Consciousness can focus on the presence in the flesh of an object only because it is first capable of tending toward something; far from the tendency being reduced to an advance toward the object, consciousness can focus on the presentation of an object only because it is fundamentally tension and aspiration. Thus Husserl's description reveals, in a way unbeknownst to him, that the intentional focus cannot be reduced to a dynamic objectivation since the latter is itself conceivable only on the basis of a desire of which it is henceforth only a modality. In short, it is not because we stand originarily in relationship with a world of objects that we are capable of focusing on it actively; on the contrary, it is because we are originarily desire and therefore open to an alterity that there can be objects for us. Husserl's analysis puts us on the path toward a determination of the originary sense of perceptual intentionality; the "fundamental movement" that within the living subject accounts for perceptual activity, insofar as it implies itself an automovement, *must be understood as desire.*[4] The opening of the world inherent in the structure of appearing relies on an originary desire, one deeper than any circumscribed incompleteness and whose scope exceeds and conditions the order of the object. Only desire can correspond to the horizon, as the presentation of the unpresentable, insofar as desire's "object" is given to it only in the mode of incompleteness and therefore always calls forth a new satisfaction.

It remains to state precisely what we understand by desire, and as the foregoing analysis of perception in Bergson suggested, it must be distinguished from need. Desire has an important characteristic: the object that satisfied it intensifies it to the exact degree that it satisfies it, so that satisfaction signifies the reactivation of desire rather than its extinguishment. As Lévinas states, the desired object does not fulfill desire but hollows it (we should add, fulfills because it hollows it). In this regard, desire is indeed distinct from need that is fulfilled by its object, that ceases with satisfaction. Need refers to a definite lacking; it aims at restoring vital completion, which is why it is always a need for something determinate. Desire, on the other hand, is not based on a lacking and strictly speaking it does not lack anything. The aspiration that animates it is not the reverse side of an absence; it exceeds vital necessities and is pure overflowing. Nevertheless, to affirm that desire does not lack anything is not to reduce it to some state of fulfillment or closure; on the contrary, it is to recognize *that nothing can fulfill it*, that the positivity of its affirmation is synonymous with an absolute dissatisfaction that no determinate object can appease. Desire thus refers to an originary incompleteness that exceeds everything that can satisfy it, that is renewed to the exact degree that it is fulfilled, and that is undoubtedly at the origin of need. One would therefore need to reverse the traditional order of dependence between these two terms: desire would not be a capricious and optional aspiration that is added to the necessities of need, but rather this originary overflowing, which runs deeper than any incompleteness, of which need would only be the deficient and finite form. Thus, far from life consisting of the satisfaction of needs, needs would be a manifestation of life as pure aspiration, originary noncoincidence. Everything happens as if the object of desire were destined to be split in two: the object providing satisfaction is given suddenly as being incomplete vis-à-vis what was truly aimed at in it, sketching the true object beneath the surface of (and absent from) desire. To say that the characteristic of desire is that the desired object fulfills it only by inflaming it is to say that its object is never fully engaged, that the correlative presence of desire is at the same time a lack of presence. That which desire covets and that which satisfies it are therefore given in its very presence as the absence of what can in no way be present, which is why satisfaction is dissatisfaction; desire's excess, which is renewed in each pleasure, responds to the retreating of the desired object behind what arouses pleasure.

Husserl did not fail to notice this excess and this priority of the dimension that we could describe as "driven" over objectivating activity. As always, Husserl makes us think both about what constitutes an obstacle to a description faithful to phenomena and what allows us to overcome this obstacle. The primacy of objectivating acts makes sense only in the framework of a static analysis. The movement toward a genetic perspective that inquires into the very origin of transcendentally constituted formations of meaning leads to profound modifications, and especially to questioning the primacy of objectivating acts. If the sense of objectual being must itself be the object of a genesis, the analysis has to clarify a type of act that owes nothing to it. This is first visible on the level of an analysis of drive, the study of which runs throughout Husserl's work. The theory of the primacy of objectivating acts shows in this precise case that an object cannot be desired if it is not first represented, and consequently that there cannot be givenness of something by drive itself.

Moreover, it is what Husserl abandons at the beginning of the 1920s. Desires, tendencies, instincts, and drives involve a singular and autonomous intentionality that is irreducible to any objectivating. We have here a relationship to something that cannot be an object. Even if desire concerns an object, what it aims at specifically is of a different order. Being hungry, for example, is not representing a thing to oneself that can be present or absent, empty or intuited intentionality; it is aiming at something in the mode of incompleteness. It must not therefore be said that a thing is missing but that in hunger a thing is given as what is missing; absence is a specific mode of manifestation and not the simple negation of a presence. This is what Husserl means when he writes, "Empty consciousness as non-filled, instinctive consciousness is not yet a consciousness that represents emptily."[5] Thus this type of intentionality gives absence in a mode that is not that of empty intentionality, commanded by the object; it is in a way absence that leads toward the object rather than the object that disappears. It should nevertheless be noted that Husserl chooses the example of need to clarify a nonobjective, autonomous intentionality, and therefore desire strictly speaking must be distinguished from it. If it is true that in the case of need the object is given in the mode of absence, it is nevertheless true that this absence is the absence of a determinate object and therefore that it can give rise to a presentation that consists here in consumption. On the contrary, even though "the object" of desire is given also in the mode of absence, this absence does not refer to a definite object. It is the absence of what cannot be presented as an object; the object of desire is what can never be present *as such*. Thus, even when a reality susceptible to satisfying it is effectively present, it is aimed at in the mode of absence, apprehended as *absent from itself*, which is why desire can never consume its object.

What is important here is that the demonstration of the autonomy of driven intentionality opens the way to a genetic dependence of objectivating intentionality vis-à-vis desire. In the texts devoted to passive synthesis,

Husserl inquires into the constitution of the originary *hylé* (*Urhylé*), which is genetically the first form in which the world is given, the access to the "there is" as such. This originary matter is given, Husserl says, in an affection, and it is therefore a question of understanding the type of intentionality and thus of originary subject (*Vor-Ich*) to which this affection corresponds. Moreover, Husserl writes: "Let us consider the thing based on hyletic domains and in particular based on quasi-extensive hyletic fields. We have here for example, the optical field and in it data detached as affecting. This does not mean that an originary interest is directed on them, on themselves: that they affect signifies that they are *terminus a quo* of driven intentions." He specifies elsewhere, in the interrogative mode, "Is not the originary affection a drive as mode of empty aspiration, still devoid of the 'representation of the objective,' aspiration that is fulfilled in a corresponding revealing act?"[6]

Thus to say that something affects me is to recognize that an indeterminate aspiration opens up a field of originary transcendence; *the activity characteristic of passivity is desire*. Desire is the test of pure dispossession. It possesses only what dispossesses it; it is rejoined only in being called by an other. The birth of a "self" and the emergence of a pure exteriority do not constitute an alternative; desire is the realized identity of an autoaffection and a heteroaffection. Husserl therefore recognizes in this context the true dimension of desire as exceeding all finite expectation. Because it is concerned only with absence and is not strictly speaking the desire of nothing ("empty aspiration"), it is not closed on a determinate quality, which is why it can receive pure matter. As the intention of a presence that is in principle unpresentable, desire opens up the pure transcendence of the world; its inextinguishable thirst is pure reception. Desire unfolds the unassignable distance from whence can emerge an affecting and an affected; it is the originary transcendental, the a priori of the affecting. Thus the genetic perspective corresponds to a total reversal of the theses derived from static phenomenology; insofar as it opens up the distance of the world, unfolds an originary transcendence that is not that of the object, "drive" (this is Husserl's term) lies at the heart of intentionality, and there is an objectivating act only subordinated to this nonobjectivating act. Correlatively, we must conclude from this that in its most originary sense the subject is life since it is ultimately in the "drivenness" of drive that the manifestation of something is rooted. As Husserl himself points out, the drive for self-preservation (which characterizes life) is simultaneously the "drive for

worldliness," in the sense in which the "fulfillment" of "the driven intentionality of monads" is "directed towards the world."[7] Desire is fundamentally the desire for the world; the life of the living subject is accomplished
only as an unfolding of a world, and there is a world only for a living. As
Montavont expresses it so well:

Drive becomes in genetic philosophy the originary form of intentionality, that
which relativizes the potencies of the objectivating act and calls into question the
perceptual model of intentionality. The latter is expressed in the 1920s less in terms
of gaze than of force: the driven being-directed-towards is less the trajectory of the
gaze than the dynamism of a force that draws the driven subject to itself. What is
important is not that Husserl accords intentionality to drive, but on the contrary,
that intentionality is now seen defined by drive: its movement is no longer that of
perceptual process but that of aspiration to (*streben nach*) according to more or less
raised degrees of intensity. The orientation of the gaze is a function of the intensity of an affective force that throws the driven subject into the encounter with the
affecting subject, and therefore with itself by way of detour through the other.[8]

Such conclusions, if they are fully accepted, lead to a destabilization of
Husserl's philosophy by threatening its very foundations. To affirm that
originary affection refers to drive is to recognize that transcendentality is
rooted in an irreducible facticity, that the very sense of the transcendental
implies its inscription in the empirical in the form of life. Insofar as it is
drive and therefore life, the subject always already precedes itself and thus
belongs to the world it opens up; the transcendental is older than itself or
delayed with regard to itself, and life is the expression of this originary delay. One could say, as has already been emphasized here, that the subject is
part of the world it conditions and that life names the constitutive arch-
facticity of the transcendental, the mutual envelopment of the world and
its condition of phenomenalization.

However, Husserl does not assume these consequences, which, as has
been seen, are in reality the phenomenological conditions for conceiving of
subjectivity as life. Driven intentionality is conceived of by Husserl as susceptible of becoming the object of a resumption in a voluntary activity,
such that the passivity of the drive is brought back to the passivity or la-
tency of a will. Far from opening up a heterogeneous dimension to the autonomy of the will, drive would be its prefiguration. Correlatively, according to the same teleological model that consists in projecting the end in the
origin under an unconscious or latent form, the opening up to an indeterminate transcendence that characterizes drive is not interpreted as a ques-

tioning of the objectivating function of intentionality; on the contrary, in desire is promised an interest in knowledge, its indeterminate aspiration is in reality curiosity, and it can therefore be accomplished only by being transformed into an activity of objectivating.

Thus in the overflow of a desire that opens to the indeterminacy of a world is promised the frontal and disinterested relation of knowledge to the object that is in itself determinable, though in the form of a *telos* that, if it is situated in the infinite, does not (because it is situated as it is) confer any less its true meaning on this originary intentionality revealed by genetic analysis. By turning to teleology Husserl reinscribes in the originary horizon of his research results that are in reality liable to shake it to the foundations; according to a recurring gesture, phenomenological rigor leads him to reveal horizons whose destabilizing power he must stifle immediately by minimizing their scope. Instead of recognizing that the originary character of desire leads to positing a constitutive inscription of the transcendental in facticity, he interprets this facticity itself as the prefiguration of the constitution of the object of knowledge by a consciousness in full possession of itself. The discovery of the originary drive is not understood as an invitation to reinterpret the meaning of the transcendental; it leads only to recognizing in it a latent mode of existence in an origin that is given as empirical. Instead of recognizing a final facticity of the transcendental, he transcendentalizes facticity itself.[9]

It should be pointed out, however, that the scope of the discovery of desire as the originary form of intentionality is not limited to a questioning of the objectivism of Husserlian phenomenology. Desire certainly reveals a type of opening to the primitive presence that escapes the framework of objectivation, but this does not mean that the order of originary experience is foreign to that of knowledge, nor that no continuity can be established between life and knowledge. The price to pay for the elucidation of the originary must not be the impossibility of establishing a passage between living and knowing. On the contrary, it seems that in determining the subject as desire—in contrast with need—we give ourselves the means of renewing the meaning of knowing, of effecting a kind of reduction of it, and therefore of conceiving of the continuity of these two dimensions. The fact that the objectivating activity is not prefigured in desire does not preclude desire from being able to bear within it the possibility of knowledge according to its true meaning.

Our question bears on the nature of the subject of appearance as an intraworldly subject. This subject is characterized by a specific form of negativity corresponding to the negativity that is indistinct from the positive and constitutive of the distance from the world, from the presence in a horizon. This negativity refers itself to a fundamental dynamic, to an originary movement that accounts for living movements seen to be constitutive of perception. The return to phenomenology as Husserl understood it in its genetic phase allowed us to clarify a primordial desire at the heart of intentionality, a desire that resembles the a priori of passivity and therefore the very condition of the world's transcendence. This desire qualifies the originary sense of the subject, and as the existential (we should say *vital*) aspect of perception it constitutes the answer to the question. We must now therefore put this hypothesis to the test, from the double point of view of rooting desire in the constitution of the living subject and its ability to account for characteristics of perception that have been identified, particularly for its originary relation to movement. If the subject of perception is indeed the living subject and if desire constitutes the existential aspect of perception, it is in truth because desire is itself constitutive of the living subject. Thus a more precise characterization of the living subject is called for here.

The advantage of the tradition established especially by Goldstein is to have taken the recognition of the living subject's specificity as its point of departure, without relying on any vital principle that names the difficulty rather than resolving it; this is why his approach, nourished as it is in other respects by gestalt psychology, fits with that of phenomenology.[10] Thus, as the study of the consequences of brain lesions shows, the living subject is characterized by the fact that it exists as a *totality*. A specific behavior takes on meaning only in relationship to the organic whole; it responds to the stimuli of the outside world only in accordance with the characteristic norms of this organism. It is therefore the living subject itself that circumscribes the field of what is efficient, susceptible to triggering a behavior. The environment, as the ensemble of that to which the organism is sensitive, is therefore constituted by the organism without, of course, this constitution relying on a distinct faculty of acts by which the living subject acts within this environment. It unfolds its world in the very movement by which it advances toward the stimuli that it contains; it makes the world appear by moving about within it. It has been seen that the living subject forms a totality with its environment in which it is legitimately impossible to distinguish what stems specifically from the organism and what comes from the outside world, to discern a dimension of passivity that would not already be marked by activity.

To the degree that this totality is not based on a vital principle that would confer on it unity and coherence despite incursions from outside, it is maintained as such and preserves the equilibrium that characterizes it only by its active relation to its environment. It is itself only in and through this dynamic exchange with the outside world; it is the conquest and conservation of the self through the mediation of the other. One could say that it involves a totality in the process of becoming, not only in the sense that it is effectively immersed in becoming (which is evident) but insofar as it *consists* in a becoming. The identity of the organism merges with the ensemble of acts and behaviors by which the relationship with the environment is established; it is merely the unity of style or manner that is manifested in each of them. The unity of the organism is not unity in spite of a becoming but in and through this becoming in which its relationships to its environment are developed. This is summed up in what Goldstein himself calls the "fundamental biological law": "the possibility of affirming itself in the world, while at the same time preserving its singularity, is linked to a certain debate (*Auseinandersetzung*) between the organism and the surrounding world, to a determined way of interacting between them."[11] It follows that what the tradition, most often blind to the specificity of the living subject, considered to be constitutive, and in particular to be the difference between the psychic and the corporeal, are only moments of this totality, generic ways of conserving a coherence with the environment. The corporeal and the psychic are no longer substances but modes of existing; they have no other reality than that of the organism itself. This is what allows Goldstein to state: "We call consciousness a mode of the human being's determined behavior as well as the generic concept of all the phenomena that are included in it. It does not involve therefore a recipient in which there would truly be determined contents. In the presence of a particular phenomenon, it is better not to say that we are conscious, but that we have a consciousness of something."[12]

Human behaviors cannot be qualified as such by the fact that they issue from a consciousness, that is, from lived experiences; but on the contrary, their conscious being refers to their humanity as the mode of the specific behavior of a living totality. This point is crucial because it allows us to renew in a profound way the approach to the problem of perception. As Erwin Straus has pointed out particularly well, for an entire tradition that extends to Husserl, perception is never referred to its effective subject, which is the living human person; it is constructed by means of a law of logical simplicity, which has nothing to do with phenomenological simplicity based on simple sensations. We find ourselves then necessarily confronted by the unsolvable problem of the relation that takes place between these sensations and their object. Moreover, we cannot claim to rigorously define perception if we do not ask ourselves first *who* perceives; it is from the mode of existence proper to this "who" that the nature of perception proceeds. Straus responds to the question in this way: "We conceive of sensation as a mode of the living-being."[13] From a perspective that is close to Goldstein's, he inscribes perceptual experience in the vital existence that characterizes the perceiving subject. The living subject does not have sensations with whose aid it would relate to the world; it *is* originarily a relationship to the world, and sensing *is a modality of this relationship*. Thus the characterization of the nature of perception does indeed refer to that of the living subject itself.

To arrive at what characterizes the living subject, at its life, it is necessary to go beyond the level of the individual. Here we must respect the methodological (but also metaphysical) principle that, by his own admission, dominates all of Goldstein's research: "the conviction that what is more perfect is never understood on the basis of what is less so, but that on the contrary, what is imperfect is understood on the basis of what is more perfect. Certainly, isolating parts of a whole is possible, but never composing the whole based on the parts."[14] In this way, the refusal of any analytical point of view and the determination of the living subject as irreducible totality are ultimately justified. However, by virtue of this principle, this determination is destined to be relativized. Since the living subject indicates a dimension of imperfection, it must be approached from the point of view of the perfection to which this imperfection refers; the totality that constitutes its being must be inscribed in a totality of a superior order. It is certainly in this way that we must understand this conclusive note, which seems extremely important to us:

Each creature expresses, in a way, both a perfection and an imperfection. Considered in an isolated way, it is in itself perfect, structured, living; in relationship to the totality, it is imperfect to different degrees. The individual creature demonstrates, in relationship to the totality of being, the same species of being that presents an isolated phenomenon of the organism in relationship to the totality of the organism: it presents imperfection, rigidity and has being only in the totality. . . .

This imperfection is expressed by individuality and stems from the artificial separation of the individual from the whole of being.[15]

Thus, insofar as it contains imperfection, organic totality must be understood by starting from a totality of a superior order.

Just as such a part or modality of the organism owes its reality only to the organic totality of which it is a part, the organism itself refers in essence to a totality that includes it; it implies in its being a reference to the whole of being. The organism is endowed with a relative perfection. It exists as totality and demonstrates an autonomy certainly superior to that of a moment of the organism, such as a reflex (to use Goldstein's example); it is not part but individual, or rather—because its individuation is not total and implies a profound dependence on the world—its individuation is of a degree superior to that of a part of itself. However, this perfection is at the same time an imperfection and in proportion to its own perfection; this separation vis-à-vis the originary totality in which its being ultimately resides is in effect correlative of its individuality, of its existence as a living subject so that this separation is in principle insurmountable.

Because it is "artificial," and hence expressing a lack of being, the separation of the individual from the whole is at the same time constitutive of its individuality, so that the individual's autonomy has as its opposite the alienation of its essence. This is tantamount to saying that the organism's being consists in lacking its being, in being separated from its own essence. Because the organism's imperfection does not correspond to a purely abstract existence within a real totality, like such an organic moment, but envelops a form of perfection while not excluding autonomy, this imperfection is inscribed in its existence. The organism is the only being that exists in the mode of incompleteness, that can be only by remaining separated from itself, excluded from its own essence. The accomplishment of perfection to which its imperfection refers would mean, for the living subject, its disappearance by dissolution in the totality (this is moreover why death is ambiguous: end and accomplishment, annihilation and deliverance). The living subject exists, lives, only to the degree that it remains withdrawn from its own essence, to the degree that it is lacking in itself; far from the living subject's existence being the realization of its essence, it can exist only as that whose essence remains unrealizable.

Such is undoubtedly the difference between the living subject and other bodies: the latter remain in calm continuity with the whole, while the living subject, making itself a totality, can relate to the originary totality only in the mode of absence. Moreover, if it is true that every living subject aims at the realization of its being, as Goldstein explicitly points out, we can conclude from this that its very existence unfolds effectively as an attempt at the reduction of this tension, of this constitutive negativity; the dynamic characteristic of existence consists in the accomplishment of its essence. This accomplishment takes the form of a relation to the totality as such, of an actualization of the "whole of being" in which lies the perfection of the living subject, which is why it remains just as much un-accomplishment since this relation is separation. *The existential autonomy* that characterizes the living subject, its aptitude to reconstitute itself and to move constantly, is therefore *the counterpart of its essential heteronomy*; it is because the living subject is separated from itself and because this separation is constitutive that all life is characterized by an unceasing dynamism. Its creative power, a concrete negativity, is the opposite of a constitutive negativity, as the absence of the totality it also is.

The living of the living subject is rooted ultimately in the fact that it aims to realize the unrealizable, to constitute a totality that is untotalizable since its own existence as living subject has as a condition the absence of this totality; the living subject is a being that relates to itself in the mode of incompleteness because it can relate to the totality only in the mode of absence. Everything stems from the fact that in constituting itself as a whole the living subject rejects outside of itself the whole of which it is a part; it alienates itself from the world, which is why harmonious continuity becomes tension. However, it is from this tension that the relation is born, from this rejection that the phenomenal being of the world emerges. Thus the living subject is a being whose being consists in being in relation to an originary totality that Goldstein calls "the whole of being," but in such a way that in this relation the totality always disappears; the lack of being that characterizes the living subject and the constitutive negation of the totality are mutual opposites.

Finally, it should be added that such negation does not signify only the limitation of a totality that would be legitimately actualizable as such; correlative to the living subject's individuality, negation is constitutive of a totality such that it is simultaneously the positing of what it is the negation of. It is within these limits that the totality is revealed as what exceeds it. The finite is by no means conceivable as the negation of an infinite; on the contrary, it is the finite that unfolds the infinite of which it is the negation. Totality that is nothing more than the world as an originary encompassing can appear only in what negates it and therefore is presented always only as the unpresentable.

It follows from this analysis that the living subject is *essentially desire*. If we understand by desire, as has been pointed out here, not a circumscribed incompleteness to which there corresponds a definite object but an incompleteness that is hollowed out by what fulfills it and that experiences every satisfaction as the negation of what would truly fulfill it, then the living of the living subject is nothing more than the act of desire. Desire is neither a derivative nor a sublimated form of need that assumes vital consistency; rather, it names the living subject's very mode of existing as essential inconsistency. Insofar as it is alienated from itself in an absent totality, the living subject has no desires; it *is* desire. Because the individuation of the living subject is the counterpart of a separation, it is not a substance; on the contrary, it is the negation of any substantiality in an active quest, or rather as this quest. Need is a missing of a part of the self and thereby assumes a constituted identity, but desire proceeds from an inconsistency and is therefore always simultaneously desire of the self. Thus in desire the relationship to the self and the relationship to the other do not constitute an alternative; the actualization of the whole in finite experiences is at the same time the constitution of the self.[16] Moreover, since it is a living subject that perceives, it is in desire, as Husserl anticipated, that the last possibility of perception must reside, and it is therefore in it that the originary unity of *Leben* and *Erleben* is intertwined.

The transitivity of experiencing refers to the constitutive transitivity of living as relationship to the totality: it is because *Leben* is originarily desire that it is just as much *Erleben*. In other words, to conceive of the subject of perception as living being and no longer as consciousness, as Straus wanted to do, is to understand that there is experience, whatever it may be, only as a modality of a relation to an originary totality. In a significant way, Straus defines from the outset the living subject (subject of sensing) as an individual "that has the power . . . to connect itself to the totality of the world."[17] He is led thereby to characterize experience as the test of a *limit* that must be understood in its specific sense. If all experience unfolds on the basis of a "relation to totality" (a constitution of a totality with the totality of the world) that it actualizes, it is clear that totality as such is never given; since it is an encompassing totality it remains untotalizable. It follows, as has been seen, that it is attained only as being missed in an experience that actualizes it, that this negation of the whole of the world that a singular experience represents is at the same time its manifestation. In experience is given in the mode of absence the whole that is its condition; in the finite is revealed the basis of which it is the specification.

This is tantamount to saying that every experience is the test of a limit in the sense that within the limit is manifested the possibility of its surpassing, is circumscribed the beyond of which it is the threshold. To grasp the given as limit is to apprehend the given as emerging from a basis that it articulates, as a moment of a totality that is its condition and that disappears in it; within the limit are born conjointly both the world and what negates it, and this is why the limit is synonymous with the horizon as the concrete form of the a priori. As Straus writes:

The relationship of totality is a potential relationship that is actualized in individual sensations and is specifically limited. By moving, the individual subject pushes itself beyond its own boundaries only to find itself enclosed by new ones. From a given *hic et nunc*, it passes into another, and the latter belongs to each sensation and to each movement. The *hic et nunc* actualize, limit and specify the relationship of totality.[18]

Upon reflection, these consequences stem from the decision to base the subject of perception on lived experience. The idea outlined by both Goldstein and Straus of a relationship to totality by no means stems from an arbitrary metaphysical position; it is simply a logical thematization of a phenomenological necessity. To identify the perceiving subject with the living subject is to abandon the idea of a consciousness that constitutes the perceived on the basis of lived experiences—in other words, to abandon the hypothesis of a specific material of perception, a material that can consist, even for Husserl, only in contents of sensation. It is these contents that confer on perception its actuality and allow it to be separated from the background. Here the determination of the perceived has a positive significance; it refers to the presence of qualitative contents. Moreover, to abandon this perspective is tantamount to inverting purely and simply the problem's givens: it is a matter of conceiving of perception as based on the perceived, of accounting for the determination of the perceived without relying on a material and specific act that creates its synthesis.

The solution consists in conceiving of *this determination as negation,* therefore in understanding the perceived as limitation of a preliminary totality and perception as a modality of a more originary relation—whence the necessity of recognizing within the living subject a constitutive dimension that connects it to the totality of the world and therefore the necessity of grasping it itself as moment of a superior dimension. Thus the definition of the living subject as a being possessing its being outside itself is correlative to the characterization of perception as the determinative negation of the totality of the world. Perception must be conceived of as a limitation rather than as a constitution to the exact degree to which the living subject refers essentially to a superior totality and contains a kind of ontological defect. It is what Bergson observes when he points out that there is less in representation than in presence, that a singular perception stems from a *découpage*, from a limitation within the whole of the images. Nevertheless, because he still conceives of the living subject as a being of need, whose dynamism is exhausted in reconstituting its integrity, he refuses to account for the whole whose perception is a negation insofar as this whole has no other reality except that which determines it and therefore is strictly only the whole *of the images*.

As has been seen, the totality of the images is conceived of as a reality based on itself. Bergson fails to account for perception at the level of the first chapter since the living subject that makes the image appear cannot simultaneously make the background against which it stands out appear. Need reveals the organism's *boundaries*; it cannot circumscribe *limits*. On the contrary, by characterizing the living subject as the desire that qualifies its originary relation to the whole of being, we provide ourselves with the means of conceiving rigorously of perceptual determination as negation, without giving ourselves what it negates in the realist mode. Desire is a test of totality in the mode of absence; it grasps the whole only in what limits it, which is why any finite satisfaction is frustration, why any experience is the desire for another experience. It is strictly speaking the *subject of the horizon*, insofar as it attains something only through what exceeds it and opens in a way upon the infinite.

Desire is the very test of the limit. Thus it is because it is the subject of desire, or rather desire as subject, that the living subject is capable of perception; it unfolds the totality whose image (the perceived) is the negation, and this in accordance with its meaning, which is to say, as unpresentable totality. The living subject is the true subject of perception since it unfolds through a single act the determinate perceived and the totality, the negation and what it negates. It opens the horizon, the originary "there is" from which spring conjointly perception and the whole of the world.

For this inquiry into the being of the intraworldly subject, we have taken as our point of departure the relation, phenomenally affirmed, between perception and movement. Henceforth, this relation no longer presents any difficulties. It is fully justified by desire as a test of the limit; representation and displacement are manifestations of this originary movement that is at the root of phenomenalization. Insofar as there is perception only as the limitation of a totality it indicates, all perception calls forth essentially its surpassing and therefore gives rise to a movement. Von Weizsäcker expresses it well when he states that "perceiving is fundamentally always passing to something else."[19] We must not only understand by this that perception can give rise to a surpassing toward another perception, but that perception *consists* in passing to something else because, insofar as it is desire, a reality can be given to it only as lacking itself and calling forth consequently a movement of surpassing. The perceived is the surpassed. However, inversely, to the degree that the totality toward which every finite moment looks possesses no reality outside these moments, there is movement only as grasped in a perception, only as being supported by it and returning to it. This is tantamount to saying that the surpassing is itself finite and that the aspiration to totality can take the form only of a passage from one state of rest to another, from one perception to another. If it is true that the perceived is grasped in a movement of surpassing, this movement itself is nevertheless still retained in perceptual manifestations and continues to be an intraworldly movement. It is this movement that Straus characterizes by the concept of *approach*,[20] the exploration that attains the thing only as still retained at a distance and therefore is given new impetus by each of the perceptions to which it gives rise. One can certainly say that phenomenal movement corresponds to the tension of desire towards totality and that perception corresponds to the finite form that the realization of this desire takes, but then we would still be speaking abstractly. Insofar as desire attains totality only in missing it and insofar as the manifestation is therefore the unity of an actualization and a negation, perception and movement pass into one another; perception and movement are two abstract expressions of a fundamental movement. Desire is merely this "I can" that is at the origin of any action and is restored to the degree that it is exteriorized—this potency that, being more profound than any action, possesses no other reality than that of its actualizations. Desire is the tension that establishes the autonomy of movement, the unassignable excess beyond the self that defines living movement.

By characterizing the subject of appearance as living and the mode of existing as desire, we satisfy the conditions of appearance that we set forth at the end of Chapter 3. We said that, by virtue of the structure of belonging, every manifestation envelops the comanifestation of a world as the preliminary foundation of presence. This manifestation implies the presence of a subject that, if it does not escape the law of appearance and therefore belongs to the world, must then be conditioning for the manifestation according to its double dimension. Moreover, such is precisely the status of the living subject as desire: though intraworldly, it unfolds conjointly the distance from the world and what is detached from it. Desire is what relates one to the other, the finite manifestation and the comanifestation of the world that it presupposes. To say that perception is desire is to say that every being appears only as the manifestation of an ultimate appearing that itself never appears. Desire unfolds the constitutive distance of the sensible; by aspiring to the totality, it opens the depth of appearance.[21] It is therefore on this basis that we can truly give meaning to the givenness by adumbrations that in our view constitutes Husserl's major discovery. On the one hand, by opening up the depth of the world desire accomplishes the function of manifestation, accounts for the adumbrating of the adumbration. On the other hand however, since it remains dissatisfaction, this depth remains concealed in the manifestation, the appearing disappears from its manifestation, and the adumbration remains an adumbration, also an evasion. To conceive of adumbrating on the basis of desire is to give ourselves the means of understanding that the absence of the adumbrated in the adumbration does not constitute an alternative to its presence and that there is manifestation only as a recoil in depth. Thus desire names this concrete negativity, which corresponds to the sense of the world's being as the immediate identity of the negative and the positive. Liberated by the reduction of positive nothingness, the negativity of the "there is" is merely the subsiding interior distance, the constitutive indeterminacy of the appearing. This is a kind of inner weakness, a kind of visible nostalgia that is prescience and expectation of a more powerful form of itself and that can have as its subject only a being existing in the mode of dissatisfaction. If the world is given originarily as horizon, the specific manifestation of the infinite unpresentable, its manifestation can be polarized only by a desire. To the objectivating intentionality that fills the emptiness of its aspiration with the object "as it is in itself" and therefore exists as consciousness, one contrasts an intentionality that fills its emptiness only by hollowing it out, that thus opens up the depth of a world and that can exist only as life.

The apparently contradictory status of the subject of appearance, inscribed in the world and condition of its manifestation, is clarified a little better when one grasps it precisely on the level of living. Insofar as the subject is desire, it relates to the whole of being and therefore is the condition of the world; however, insofar as desire has no other reality than that of the movements to which it gives rise, insofar as its aspiration becomes exploration, it is contained in the world it reveals. By its very essence, desire is destined to be dispersed in finite tendencies—which can even include needs; its transcendental dimension implies its empirical becoming, which is why there is desire only as life. But there is desire only as life because there is constituted being of the world only as all-encompassing and therefore simultaneously unconstitutable; the passivity of desire corresponds to the untotalizable transcendence of the world. Thus, opening conjoined with the manifestation and with its withdrawal in the distance, desire is the originary unity of passivity and activity; it possesses the world only as what dispossess it. Because the living subject exists only by remaining within its being, it unfolds the totality only in the form of what negates it and therefore contains the world only as what contains it: desire is the fact of the transcendental, or rather the transcendental as fact, the concrete form of its originary delay. Such is, in our view, the true significance of the chiasma by which in the final analysis Merleau-Ponty defined phenomenality. If the flesh is indeed what is itself affected only by being affected by another, this "encompassing-encompassed" that contains what contains it, then desire constitutes the sense of being proper to the flesh.

This determination of phenomenality leads to a renewed theory of ipseity, of the psychophysical duality and of the unconscious. To define the subject as desire is to conceive of it as identity realized from presence to self and absence of self. Thus, although we agree with Michel Henry in conceiving of the subject as life, we think that, for this very reason, it cannot be characterized as pure autoaffection. If it is true that desire is at the heart of life, then the autoaffection that characterizes the subject has meaning and reality only as heteroaffection; the closure of the *ipse* does not form an alternative to the opening up of a distance, its affective immanence to a form of impenetrableness. On the other hand, it follows from these conclusions that the psychophysical duality must be abandoned, in whatever form, and consequently we must understand the body and the soul as simple modalities of life, as phases or moments of the desire that constitutes it as life.

If it is true that the living subject is indeed an irreducible reality, then we can no longer conceive of desire as a property of the body. The latter stems, on the contrary, from an incarnation that is itself inherent in desire insofar as it implies a dimension of finitization or withdrawal into the self and therefore can be related only to worldly objects. Correlatively, the soul would merely be *the body's excess*, an overflowing of the self, a dissatisfaction vis-à-vis any finite realization that characterizes desire. The duality of the soul and the body is therefore essentially derivative and relative; the soul and the body are distinguished only as the aspiration that animates desire and its finite actualization, which is tantamount to saying that they are the same. Their duality disappears before the dynamic unity of life and ultimately corresponds only to the tension of the desire that is in its heart.

We could show, finally, that this perspective allows us to reveal a concept of the unconscious that totally escapes the order of representation to which Freud still subjected it and whose significance is therefore ontological rather than psychological. If the unconscious is rooted in desire, as Freud demonstrated definitively, it has as content no longer representation but the world itself; it is *in front of us* and not *in us*, as Merleau-Ponty points out. It corresponds to this untotalizable totality, this invisible that each perception simultaneously actualizes and misses by repelling it into the depths. The unconscious is synonymous with horizon(t)ality as the specific presentation of the originary totality, which is why it corresponds to a constitutive dimension of experience, as Freud rightly saw. The relation of the unconscious to repression (which we know is essential since Freud defines the unconscious as the repressed) is seen in a new light. Since the desired, the world, is its own withdrawal behind the manifestations of experience, repression is inherent in desire and no longer due to a process that would be exterior to it. The originary unity of manifestation and the world that is manifested in it while hiding in it accounts for the essential relation between the unconscious and repression. The Freudian topics possess an ontological meaning. The "other scene" that defines the unconscious is none other than the world's scene.

Conclusion

By way of conclusion, we would like to make three remarks that, insofar as they follow from what has been developed, constitute as many directions for the further study.

First, it is clear that the position developed here leads to a radical rethinking of the status of space and time. For the Husserlian perspective, and indeed for the quasi-totality of the phenomenological tradition, the constitutive transcendence of manifestation merges with temporal transcendence. Referring the world to the subject is ultimately constituting it in time. In Husserl, the *hylé*'s originary manifestation is based on the reserve of the past in retention and therefore merges with the autoconstitution of time; the distance inherent in manifestation is opened up by the waning of time. It is in the succession of nows that is constituted the unity of which they are the manifestation, which is tantamount to saying that time is the ultimate form of passive synthesis. In short, it is because the manifestation is temporal that it can be a manifestation of a world. Moreover, this characterization of the structure of appearance leads purely and simply to overturning this primacy of temporality. We can conclude from the preceding that belonging defines the structure of appearance, and that there is therefore manifestation only as the comanifestation of a world. In other words, there is manifestation emerging only from an all-encompassing totality that it simultaneously actualizes and conceals by its becoming present. Approached from the "subjective" perspective, this means that originary intentionality consists in a desire in which are constituted conjointly the limiting manifestation and what transcends it—the horizon as the originary form of appearance. Thus there is manifestation only insofar as it emerges from a distance or a depth, only insofar as it presents an originary totality. The latter contains in principle all that can appear to the degree that it is not unfolded as a positive element, in which it is merely what occurs in it; it merges with the horizon as presentation of the infinite. The world is the *reserve* of manifestation in the sense of both the interior distance by which it distinguishes itself and what is the potency of any possible manifestation. Everything depends therefore on the fact that the givenness of the world in the flesh is the condition of appearance, which is why there is a test peculiar to absence: the "instinctive" character of intentionality corresponds precisely to the fact that the world's presence in the flesh implies a constitutive dimension of absence. As Patočka writes: "Everything that appears, that is to say in general everything that can be experience, not only intuitively but even indirectly and in a purely conjectural way, empty and formal, can appear only because the essence of manifestation encompasses *everything*."[1]

Thus there is manifestation only on the basis of a unique space, of an encompassing that, because it includes everything, is strictly speaking neither spatial nor temporal and instead conceals the respective possibility of space and time. This is why, far from representing the ultimate source of appearance, temporality itself is rooted in appearance as the givenness of a world. It is not because manifestations are temporal that they are manifestations of a world; on the contrary, it is because each manifestation is a manifestation of one and the same world that it can be temporally unified with the others. The passive synthesis (but still active insofar as it is synthesis) of time refers to a synthesis that is already achieved in things, or rather to the all-encompassing as realized synthesis. Therefore it is not because a given adumbration passes and is retained in this passing that a transcendence can appear; it is because each adumbration opens upon the unassignable transcendence of the world that it can surpass itself toward others.

Far from the horizon referring to the temporal structure of consciousness, the temporal structure of consciousness refers to the horizon as the ultimate form of being. Moreover, what is valid for time is equally valid for this other synthesis that is space (extension). It could therefore be said that these unitary forms by which the qualified content surpasses its punctuality in order to be opened up to other contents are a kind of manifestation of a more originary unity, the prespatial and pretemporal copresence of all the qualified contents within (or rather as) one and the same world. The unity in exteriority that space and time represent is based on the originary interiority of all the possible contents within the "there is."[2] As Patočka expresses it so admirably: "There must be something as a movement by which the world's heart constitutes its contingent content and whose space-time-quality in totality is a sediment."[3]

Spatial and temporal unity is only a testimony to and a trace of the originary copresence of everything that can be within the encompassing. Thus it is not because they are in space and time that things form a world; it is because they are things of the world that they can be unified according to space and time. What has always been understood as form refers in reality to the depth of foundation. The unification of things in space and time is only the mirror image of their differentiation from a basis upon which they are a single entity, one in which in reality the difference between the one and the many does not yet have meaning. It is precisely because they are always still retained in the foundation that their diversity appears according to the spatiotemporal unity. There is therefore indeed something such as an originary simultaneity by which each thing is already linked to all others and is, in truth, this very relation; each thing is there and later (or in the past) while being here and now. It is for this reason that space and time could be shown to be only the most general modalities of all manner of degrees of the relationship between the singular contents, of equivalencies without concept that are the true meaning of essence. Space, time, and essence are only modalities or levels of these "dimensions" or "rays of the world," as Merleau-Ponty calls them, of these nonthematic modes of unity, these styles that all attest to belonging to one and the same world. Space and time are not the elements in which a positive and atemporal essence would be actualized by being exteriorized, but instead the style common to everything that appears, to the most universal essence.

Because they structure the order of existence, space and time constitute the essence of essence. Nevertheless, this originary simultaneity should not be conceived of as an element unfolded outside of what occurs in it; it can be pretemporal only by being equally prespatial. Precisely because it is all-encompassing, the world cannot be unfolded outside each of the manifestations in which it is manifested. Its simultaneity therefore excludes extension; its depth defies measurement. It is a copresence without place whose unity is constituted on the level of the diversities of the manifestations. One could say that the world is correlative to a life and that its simultaneity does not constitute an alternative with succession since it is constituted in the very becoming of this life. Far from excluding each other, these two aspects are complementary. It is not in being unfolded all at once that the world can be all-encompassing; rather, in the becoming of constituting life its reserve can be preserved. All desire is desire of a world, and thereby the manifestation that proceeds from it is already unified with all the others according to an originary simultaneity. But to the degree that this desire can never be fulfilled and therefore tests the world only in what limits it, this simultaneity is synonymous with a succession and so is accomplished only as the becoming of this life. It is necessary to understand that it is not because the living subject is temporal that it is desire; it is because it is desire and therefore relates to the totality only in the mode of lacking that it unfolds as life and therefore as temporality.

Second, these remarks lead now to the most difficult question, that of the ultimate relationship between subject and appearance, between desire and distance. Beyond the objective movements of inert bodies and the intentional movements of living subjects, there exists a fundamental movement by which appearance as such is possible, which we have characterized as desire. It is from desire's own tension that living movements stem; it is what gives a more profound sense of living than the distinction between being-in-life and experiencing. It is a question of a movement in a sense already "metaphorical," because it is a tension toward, an aspiration, and by no means a displacement. According to a configuration that appears paradoxical, this intraworldly desire is the condition of manifestation of the world itself, which is precisely why we have seen in it the effective form of a delay upon self of the transcendental, something like a facticity of the transcendental. In effect, it constitutes only by letting itself be affected; it can open the world only by already entering the world and by being subjected therefore to its law: its initiative is radical passivity.

Moreover, in expressing ourselves this way, are we not demonstrating the inadequacy of our categories, derived from phenomenology in relation to what there is to consider? In referring to facticity of the transcendental, are we not naming the difficulty rather than resolving it? Otherwise stated, if the so-called constituting activity of desire is reconciled with its intraworldliness, is it not because it is not the true subject of its initiative and that in its movement is revealed a movement in an even more profound sense? This movement would be that of manifestation itself, and it would have the world as true "subject." The living of life thereby would be only the place or the point of passage of a dynamic whose initiative it does not possess. Patočka seems to anticipate this in evoking, at least once, "a proto-movement" as "going outside the obscure foundation," which is distinct from a "secondary manifestation," from "the manifestation of the appearing" that presupposes the creation of centers.[4] In other words, to affirm the autonomy of appearance is ipso facto to recognize a movement of appearance that precedes in a way its centralization by a subjective pole and that renders this centralization possible. From protomovement by which the world appears and that can have as its ultimate subject only the world itself, we would therefore need to distinguish the movement of desire as the condition on which the "going outside the obscure foundation" is crystallized in manifestation, as if the world needed life for its going out from the foundation to be transformed into a phenomenon. Thus at the heart of the subject's movement would be another "movement," that of the manifestation itself, and the living subject would be the subject of appearance only insofar as the originary movement of the world's going out of itself is accomplished as life.

In a coherent way, then, the intraworldly subject would crystallize and centralize an appearance; a protomovement of which it does not possess the initiative, the subject's desire would correspond to an aspiration to an appearance that has its source in the "there is" itself. However, if this is indeed the case, are we not going beyond the strictly phenomenological context in favor of what we could call a cosmology? Ricœur characterizes cosmology as the existence of "a universe of discourse that would be 'neutral' with respect to objectivity and subjectivity," as the possibility of a "material ontology common to the region of nature—known by external perception and objective natural sciences—and to the region of consciousness known by reflection and by phenomenology of the subject."[5] Now, it is clear that desire, just as the movement of manifestation, is movement in the same sense, seemingly metaphorical but undoubtedly foundational for all others and therefore in reality characteristic as the *actualization of a potency that is indefinitely renewed by this actualization*, an actualization which, not relying on a constituted subject and therefore not polarized by a preliminary essence, has as its purpose only the very renewal of the potency. It is this movement, which is deeper than the distinction between the movement of life and that of manifestation—namely, the movement that establishes the possibility of speaking about a "life" of manifestation—that Merleau-Ponty undoubtedly had in mind when he evoked in his final working notes, regarding this absolute that is the sensible, "one sole explosion of Being that is forever," a "stabilized explosion."[6] Stabilized explosion because it is the actualization of a basis that still retains it in its depth and therefore can never fall outside its explosion in the form of fully positive beings, the actualization of that whose infinity excludes all true passing over to act, which is why the explosion of being is "forever."

Inevitably, Aristotle comes to mind when trying to outline the sense of cosmology in this context. It can certainly be said, regarding the theory of act and potency, that it stems from an anthropoligization of being, from a projection of the structures of life and action onto natural reality. But we can also interpret Aristotle's physics and metaphysics a little less naively as the attempt to clarify a sense of change that is neutral vis-à-vis the distinction between the anthropological and the physical, an originary structure that accounts for both the life of living subjects and that of being and therefore establishes a cosmology in the sense that Ricœur defines it. Nevertheless, since it is unquestionably governed by the primacy of *ousia*, the theory of act and potency cannot be adopted as is in order to describe movement in its originary sense. Aristotle's movement must therefore be repeated, but on the basis of a radicalization of the theory of act and potency, a radicalization that consists in suspending the primacy of substantiality in order to conceive of a movement that would no longer be movement "from something," one consequently destined to result in immobility. Patočka, who has reflected on this question more than anyone else, writes in this regard: "Movement of this kind makes us think of the movement of a melody or, more generally of a musical composition: each element is only a part of something that exceeds it, that is not then and there in a finished form, something rather that, prepared in all singularities, remains always, in a certain sense, to-come, as long as the composition is heard."[7]

This movement designates indistinctly that of desire and that of manifestation, an originary life short of the distinction between living and appearing. Thus the activity of the living subject does not contradict its passivity, since this activity is not in the final analysis *its* activity but that of the manifestation itself. There is a sense of living that is neutral in relation to the division between being in life and experiencing, but it refers to a still more originary sense, one that is neutral vis-à-vis the division between the two senses of preceding and coming to light. The life of living subjects would stem from a primordial movement, from a "going outside the obscure foundation"; it would precede itself in a nature in the post-Aristotelian sense of a being that is its own explosion. There would thus be a co-originarity of being and life, and if phenomenology opens onto a cosmology, the latter can have only the meaning of a cosmobiology.[8]

Finally, at the conclusion of this study, one question is essential: How can knowledge be accounted for? In a more general way, How can we account for the order of meanings on the basis of this analysis of perception? Perception has been separated from the reference to a positive object in order to inscribe it in life itself; however, in so doing, an insurmountable gulf may have been introduced between the order of living and that of knowing. The alternative would be between a philosophy of perception (which does not lose sight of the question of the possibility of understanding and which is therefore forced to define it teleologically from this possibility) and a philosophy that, by clarifying the rootedness of perceiving in vital activity and consequently in separating out a nucleus common to the human person and to animals, abandons the attempt to account for the rational order and thus adopts a sort of displaced Platonism. In reality, this objection is unfounded because it presupposes a certain idea of knowledge, and above all of life. Thus it is not because we regrasp perception on the basis of living that we compromise the possibility of accounting for the continuity of perceiving and knowing; rather, it is *to the degree that we conceive of living in a reductionist way as a subjugation to needs.*[9]

Such is Straus's position, for whom sensing is distinguished from perceiving as a pathic mode of existing, from a gnostic mode. In sensing, the living subject grasps immediately the object according to its vital significance, which is why sensing is not distinguished from the movement, whether approaching or fleeing, that its object provokes. As Straus recognizes explicitly, sensing is rooted in a living that is reduced to vital necessities; it responds to need: "The first stage of sensory experience is that of separation and union, whose respective cardinal forms, nutrition and reproduction, are assured by sensing."[10] Thus sensing is merely the dynamic apprehension of an object according to the sense it has for the integrity of the organism and the species (threat, food, partner). It is based therefore on a "symbiotic" understanding: riveted to vital necessities, it allows no distance vis-à-vis its object and therefore cannot even attempt a recognition or a thematization. Such is, on the contrary, the function of the perceiving that grasps the object as it is rather than according to organic needs; perception steps back in relation to the object by moving away from vital pressure and thus can grasp it thematically. Sensing is blind captivation by vital necessity and by what incarnates it; perceiving is a positing of the object and consequently consciousness of self. Thus perception is torn between a life that reacts to the thing rather than relating to it and a knowledge (perception is for Straus the first degree of knowledge) of which we ask how it can be rooted in a life. Everything happens therefore as if perception strictly speaking, as the givenness in the flesh of a transcendent reality, was missed: by default, in a symbiotic understanding—whether exclusively affective or motor—that cannot open to exteriority as such; by excess, in an opening to transcendence that merges with the positing of an object and of which we then ask how it is distinguished from an act of understanding.

Now, it is clear that this explosion of perception proceeds from a restrictive characterization of life; it is because life is understood as the ensemble of acts by which an organism maintains its integrity and that of the species. It is therefore because we refuse to root perception in living that we must finally make it depend in a rather traditional way on a thetic act. The attempt to inscribe perception in vital activity cannot succeed; sensing, as Straus understands it, cannot have the scope of a perceiving since this activity is conceived of as limited by the sphere of needs. Such an attempt demands in reality that the very meaning of living be reexamined in light of its ability to give rise to perception. Moreover, this situation stems from a decision, first thematized by Heidegger, that Henri Maldiney sums up in this way: "Nothingness is not part of life's text."[11] To define life on the basis of need, and thus not to recognize implications of instinct other than those of vital objects (food, partner, and the like), is to rivet it to pure positivity; if only what fulfills a want exists, nothingness cannot be part of the living subject's world. By defining life on the basis of need as lacking, we are led to deny it any ability to make negativity appear in the world. Incompleteness as the absence of a circumscribed object is a false negativity; it is the aspiration to fullness and not the opening up of an absence, which is why the living subject cannot unfold the depth required by perception.

Thus it is characterization of the living subject as incapable of negativity that leads to introduction of a perceptual level at odds with the order of life. This rupture corresponds precisely to the emergence of the negative, to the ability to distance oneself from what appears by breaking the object's immediate identity with itself; to seize upon the object as involving negativity, as not being what it is, is to separate it from its essence and thus to understand it as being. It could easily be shown that this conception of a living subject riveted to positivity has as a counterpart an idea of experience that itself refers to a characterization of the negative as pure nothingness. Determination of the living subject as incapable of negativity and that of the appearing as a determinable being in itself (being separated from a background of nothingness) represent two aspects of an identical philosophical attitude.[12] Be that as it may, it is indeed because the living subject is denied the aptitude toward the negative that we do not allow ourselves to conceive of the continuity between living and knowing. Inversely, it is to the degree that we introduce "nothingness in life's text" that we can truly root perception in it and thereby account for the continuity between the perceptual order and the cognitive order.

Thus to conceive of life as desire is to root in it the possibility of knowing. As was seen earlier, desire is the subject of a horizon and gives rise to a presence that contains a dimension of absence. The living subject is a being that is related essentially to the whole of the world and whose experience necessarily contains negativity; for it, absence is not the negation of presence but a mode of given, which is why it is capable of moving. Life is negativity, an unfulfillable lacking that opens up the field of transcendence within which being can appear: because it is dissatisfaction, life is also pure reception, open to presence as such. Hence negativity, which has been seen as constitutive of perception strictly speaking, is by no means the attribute of the human person and of its anguish; instead it emerges from the vital level. The living subject is not a being enclosed in the circle of need; it is dissatisfaction and therefore exists in a mode of exploration. Far from being reduced to being only what incites a reaction, the object is, for the living subject, what opens a depth and calls forth an indefinite approach for the living subject; the sense of transcendence is rooted in life.

Insofar as it is already perception, life therefore already bears within it the possibility of knowing, which certainly must be understood in a renewed sense. By understanding living beyond need, knowing is apprehended on this side of the positing of a pure object. In a sense, the study of life allows us to reduce the naïve positing of knowledge as the apprehension of positive meanings. Life is a relationship to absence and the test of presence as what cannot fulfill this absence. It is therefore on the very level of desire that what Husserl elucidated as the relationship between empty intentionality and fulfillment is constituted, but as an always unequal relationship, a constitutive impossibility of fulfilling emptiness. To say that the subject is desire is to recognize both that there is emptiness only fulfilled and that there is also always an excess of emptiness beyond fulfillment. This is tantamount to saying, as

Merleau-Ponty perceptively points out, that "it is not a positive being but an interrogative being who defines life."[13] The characteristic of questioning is that instead of concluding the debate the response renews its expectations. Thus if knowing is apprehended on the basis of the interrogative dimension that fundamentally defines it, its continuity is discovered with the vital order; questioning continues the exploration that characterizes life. Straus himself is led to recognize this despite the break that he wants to establish: "The incomplete-being in the particularity of the actual moment constitutes the fundamental ontological possibility of a transition from a *here* to a *there*, of one particularity to another. Only this existential character renders spontaneous movement possible, that is to say animal exploration and human questioning."[14]

Beyond the break between the spatial and the spiritual, desire and questioning are one and the same movement. Thus it is in the constitutive desire of life that the interrogative dimension is rooted, a dimension that is itself the heart of our knowing; here the confrontation is with a deeper dimension that we are unable to name, of which desire and questioning, life and knowledge are only modalities. The activity of thought, as the quest for a meaning that exceeds the significations in which it is crystallized, prolongs a movement that is at the very root of life. Such is unquestionably the sense of the rational teleology that Husserl observed from the originary level of drive. However, it is a teleology without a *telos*, a wanting that—not being need—lacks nothing, does not refer to a determined object, and cannot therefore be fulfilled. This is why, ultimately, there does not exist an alternative between life and philosophy; by questioning, we reappropriate our roots and make ourselves living beings.

Author's Afterword

Although I have been deeply honored to have Stanford University Press publish this English translation of *Le désir et la distance*, I confess that this project has also been the occasion for a somewhat anxious rereading of my work. With several years' distance from its original publication, I asked myself at each page whether my work is worthy of this recognition. Does it set forth a sufficient theoretical soundness and coherence to justify this potential increase in readership? Obviously, this is not for me to judge. *Desire and Distance* involves on the one hand the question of the subject's sense of being and that of the ultimate status of movement by which we have characterized this subject, and on the other hand the question of its consequences on the phenomenological character of our undertaking, the beginning and end of our approach. It is centered on the question of the perceiving subject's sense of being, of the subject of appearance insofar as this appearance is characterized by a structure of belonging or horizon. We have responded to this question by taking as our point of departure the Merleau-Pontian analysis of perception and the constitutive intertwining between perception and movement that it clearly brings to the fore following upon Goldstein or Von Weizsäcker. In so doing, we remained dependent on a still naïve determination of the perceiving subject, a determination insufficiently concerned with questioning the body's sense of being. In other words, we had not taken advantage, in this step toward movement as the perceiving subject's sense of being, of the existential analysis that, following Heidegger, emphasizes that which distinguishes the human subject from other beings. Moreover, to the degree that Patočka, starting from an analysis of the Heideggerian problematic, rediscovers precisely the identity between perception and movement, it is indeed our inquiry into the sense of being of the perceiving subject that encourages us to pursue a more thorough analysis of our reading of Patočka.

In fact, this question is subject to a number of constraints. Merleau-Ponty continually criticizes the "abyss of meaning" that Husserl establishes between transcendental consciousness and worldly reality, the fact that consciousness is without links to the world and can thus project over it through and through. Undoubtedly, because he conceived of reality's sense of being in a univocal way, Husserl can consider the difference of being of consciousness vis-à-vis worldly beings only as exteriority *in relationship to the world itself,* and this is why consciousness is understood as a sphere of absolute being. It is in opposition to this position that Merleau-Ponty develops his phenomenology of perception. We cannot retreat to the depths of nothingness to project over the world and grasp it in transparence; on the contrary, the inscription of the perceiving subject in the world corresponds to the irreducible transcendence of the perceived. The perceiving subject is *of* the world; it is inserted in it, which is why it can simultaneously attain it, by virtue of its ontological relationship with it, but not bring it to the transparence of representation precisely because of its inscription in it. However, if the perceiving subject is of the world, it cannot be for all that in the same mode as other intraworldly beings insofar as it is precisely their condition of manifestation, and insofar as it opens the world itself. The question therefore becomes more specific: What is the sense of being of the perceiving subject (of intentionality) insofar as it belongs to the world without nevertheless existing in the same mode as other beings since it is through it that they appear?

It is not certain that the Merleau-Pontian characterization of the perceiving subject accounts for the complexities of the problem. Indeed, everything proceeds as if, by disagreeing with Husserl, Merleau-Ponty still remained dependent on him and therefore extended the presuppositions that govern transcendental phenomenology. It is uncertain that in criticizing the extraworldliness of transcendental consciousness in order to bring the perceiving subject back to the level of the world we give ourselves the means of reaching its true sense of being. In fact, the risk is in maintaining the implicit presupposition in the name of which Husserl hollowed out an abyss of meaning between consciousness and reality, namely the univocality of the meaning of intraworldliness, and in conceiving then of the perceiving subject as a being among others under the pretext that it exists within the world. Such is indeed the objection to which the definition of the perceiving subject as the body itself or as flesh is exposed.

Merleau-Ponty denies the absoluteness of Husserlian consciousness and as a result insists on the necessary incarnation of perceptual consciousness more than he exhibits the sense of being of this body insofar as it is capable of perception and insofar as its passivity is therefore at the same time activity. He emphasizes the body over consciousness more than he moves beyond their duality toward a more original sense of being, and he thus extends the Husserlian impasses as he attempts to free himself from them. This is particularly striking in *The Visible and the Invisible*, in which the subject of perception is defined as touching-touched or seeing-seen. We have in this instance a purely negative characterization that constantly relies on what it supposedly criticizes: the duality between feeling and felt, between subject and object. Saying that touching is simultaneously touched, and touched insofar as it is touching, is indeed eliminating the distance between the transcendental and the empirical; it is inscribing the activity of the subject in a fundamental dimension of passivity. It is thereby recognizing that the perceptual possession of the world has as its foundation an originary dispossession that has the body as its condition—but it is also confirming duality at the very moment we are trying to overcome it. In proceeding in this manner, Merleau-Ponty draws the horizon of a mode of original existing in which this duality would be surpassed; however, this horizon is destined to remain without content since it is drawn from this very duality. To speak of flesh is to emphasize the necessity of intraworldliness for perceptual consciousness. It is to recognize that there is opening to the world only from within the world, but it is not yet determining the sense of being upon which is based the unity between feeling and its intraworldliness. The problem of intentionality is therefore formulated in the form of a problem that Merleau-Ponty does not confront radically: What is the sense of being of the perceiving subject, insofar as being intraworldly, if it does not however exist in the same mode as things? How can this singular clarity that is touch or sight take place within the world?

Heidegger's incomparable achievement is having at once gauged this difficulty and having therefore been able to reintegrate the Husserlian subject in the world without compromising for all that the difference from its sense of being.[1] *Dasein* precisely designates a being that, even though it belongs to the world, is characterized by a sense of being radically different from other worldly beings, a sense of being that Heidegger defines by the concept of *existence*: things of the world subsist and are therefore determined by categories, but *Dasein* exists and is therefore structured by existentials. To say that *Dasein* exists is to recognize that its own being is involved in this being, that it relates to its being as to its most characteristic possibility. This does not mean that *Dasein* has available possibilities from which it would already independently exist, but that it *is* its possibility, its capacity to be, and that its being merges therefore with its own realization. As Patočka points out so insightfully: "Existing in comprehension is not *representing* our being to ourselves, evoking in spirit and evaluating our projects and our intentions. Existing in comprehension is *being in possibilities*, which does not in turn signify that we represent different possibilities to ourselves, different options, but indeed that we accomplish them, we realize them, we are continually not only *in* but still *ahead of our action*."[2]

In other words, Heidegger considers that intentionality can be conceived of in accordance with its meaning only on the condition of not being referred to a being that would distinguish itself from it and that would be its subject, consciousness or body, but on the condition of being understood, on the contrary, as an ultimate and irreducible mode of being on which the subject's very identity must be based. Intentionality is not a characteristic but a specific sense of being, which is that of a dynamism: intentionality exists as accomplishment and is its realization. It is not relation of a subject to something other than itself but rather being as relationship, existence insofar as it is capacity-to-be, being ahead of self. Heidegger can therefore legitimately see in being-in-the-world the fundamental constitution of *Dasein*, the true significance of intentionality: "*Transcendence* is a *fundamental determination of the Dasein's ontological structure*. It is part of the existentiality of existence. Transcendence is an existential concept. We will see that intentionality is based on *Dasein*'s transcendence and that it is possible only on this basis, while transcendence on the other hand could not be explained based on intentionality."[3]

Nonetheless, in this instance Heidegger exposes himself to a criticism that is symmetrical to what we directed toward Merleau-Ponty. Just as Merleau-Ponty does not rise from the level of incarnation to that of the sense of being upon which perceptual intentionality could be based, Heidegger does not determine existence, authentic sense of intentionality, in such a way that its intraworldliness, its corporeality, is clearly conceivable.

We are focusing here, without being able to develop this idea more fully, on the impossibility in which Heidegger finds himself in making a place for flesh in *Dasein*'s existentials, and correlatively, in situating life, which avoids the division between *Vorhandenheit* and existence, within *Dasein*'s analytic. Thus, although Merleau-Ponty conceives of the intraworldliness of flesh such that an intentional opening cannot be based on it, Heidegger conceives of the intentional opening in such a way that its intraworldliness cannot be deduced from it.[4] Patočka, better than anyone prior to him, has gauged this limit of *Dasein*'s analytic: "It would seem that the analytic renders the Heideggerian ontology of existence too formal. The praxis is indeed the original form of clarity, but Heidegger never takes into consideration the fact that the original praxis must on principle be the activity of a *corporeal* subject, that corporeality must therefore have an ontological status that can not be identical to the body's occurrence as present here and now."[5]

Patočka recognizes here the necessity of integrating corporeality with existence, but he observes at the same time the danger represented by Merleau-Ponty of referring this corporeality to the subsisting presence, a notion that would obviously compromise the specificity of existence. This is why, if existence must indeed be referred to corporeality, the latter must itself be grasped on the *existential* level; it is on this condition only that we are able to arrive at the body's true sense of being as Merleau-Ponty indicates, without being able to thematize it. Patočka stresses the fact that the link between "the in-view-of" and what follows as a consequence of it under the species of our concrete tasks can be ensured only by the corporeality of existence. Moreover, according to Patočka, the sense of this corporeality is not fully restored by the analysis of the *Befindlichkeit* because, as he points out, facticity as it is determined by the disposition of mood is not as such anything expressly corporeal. Rather, corporeality must be understood existentially, as a possibility in which we insert ourselves but that we have not chosen:

All that I accomplish is done in view of my being, but at the same time, there is a *fundamental* possibility that must be open to me, a possibility without which all the others remain suspended in the void, without which they are devoid of meaning and unrealizable. What is primary, primordial, is therefore nothing contingent, nothing ontic, but has *as first possibility*, the basic ontological status of all existence. This is tantamount to saying that it is not one possibility among others, but rather a privileged possibility that will co-determine in its meaning existence in its entirety. This ontological basis is corporeality as *possibility of moving*.[6]

Corporeal movement—living movement—constitutes the characteristic existential determination of corporeality, and since this possibility codetermines in its meaning existence in its entirety, it constitutes the primary existential of existence insofar as this existence is incarnated. Through living movement, the dynamism of existence, which names so to speak the form of intentionality, is rendered to its intraworldliness. It follows that life loses the problematic status that it had in Heidegger's work and that the continuity between existence and life can thus be restored; if existence relies on motor corporeality, it is indeed, fundamentally, life.[7] As Patočka writes:

On the foundation of corporeality, our activity is always a movement *from . . . towards . . .* it always has a point of departure and a goal. On this foundation, our existence is always burdened, in regards to its activity, with the weight of need, of repetition, of restoration and of the prolonging of corporeality itself. The circle of existence (existing in view of oneself, in view of the mode of one's being) always contains in a certain way the circle of life that accomplishes vital functions in order to return in itself and to come back to itself—in such a way that life is the goal of all its particular functions.[8]

But thereby it is corporeality's true sense of being, thematized by Merleau-Ponty in terms of touching-touched or the unity of activity and passivity, that is revealed here. Movement designates the essence of incarnation, insofar as the latter is capable of illuminating what it is not. In effect, in recognizing (as ultimate existential) corporeality as possibility of moving, Patočka in no case comes back to a body's subsisting presence that would have the faculty or characteristic of moving. He means instead that it is *in living movement that the essence of incarnation resides*. It is not because *Dasein* has a body that it is capable of moving; it is on the contrary because its existence is essentially movement that it can be incarnated. Regarding the constitutive nature of movement vis-à-vis the body, Patočka allows no lingering doubts:

The personal body is not a thing in objective space. It is a life that, by itself, *is spatially*, that *produces* its own localization, that makes itself spatial. The personal body is not a being in the way that a thing is, but as relationship, or rather as relating to self that is the subjective relationship that it is only by making the detour through an outside being. Moreover, for this very reason, it is necessarily living body, it does not need to localize itself among things as one of them.[9]

One cannot state any more clearly that the body must be conceived of starting with life as constitution of self through a relation with beings, rather than life as a characteristic of the body, objectively conceived as organism or as support of sensory fields. The body is this being that exists in the mode of relationship and comes back to itself—constitutes itself on the basis of its entry into exteriority. The body is a temporal or historical unity that creates *itself* against what undoes it through a continual movement toward and within exteriority. Moreover, in determining the body on the basis of movement, we give ourselves at the same time the means of answering the question first raised by Merleau-Ponty of the perceiving body's ultimate sense of being: perceiving, insofar as it occurs in the midst of the world, insofar as it is incarnated, is a moving.[10] Thus conceiving of incarnation as living movement is going beyond the still abstract alternative between an existence that lacks the dimension of incarnation and a substantial corporeality about which we do not understand how it can open to a pure transcendence (perceiving). It is as living movement that *Dasein* is incarnated in accordance with its being and that the Merleau-Pontian flesh exists in accordance with its perceptual clairvoyance. Living movement is indeed the response to the question of the being of intentionality. Fully intraworldly, it is distinguished from all other beings insofar as it does not rely on itself but moves, that is to say is realized. It differs from other beings because it exists in a mode of difference with self.

Yet we must agree about the significance of this movement. It is clear that it cannot be understood in the modern and naïve sense of a simple displacement in space and therefore that the recognition of an essential incarnation of *Dasein* is itself governed by a renewed ontology of movement. Moreover, it is in confronting Aristotle's theory of movement that Patočka elaborates a concept of movement that applies to existence itself. Indeed, it is evident that movement in the sense of modern natural sciences must be set aside since they conceive of it "not as change, but as essentially quantitative mathematical structure, the basis of which is trajectory."[11] The modern conception of movement must therefore be understood as proceeding from an objectivating idealization of original movement. The latter is first approached starting with the Aristotelian definition; according to Patočka's terms, it is being-in-act of possibility, insofar as it is in possibility—in other words, actualization of potential as potential. Patočka states that "existence is a mode of being that is *the act of accomplishment of self*—that is its own goal, that through its action returns to self, that is its own act in and next to itself. Existence is thus something like a movement, and just as movement, according to Aristotle, is passage from possibility to accomplished actuality, passage that is itself accomplishing, so existence too is *life in possibility*."[12]

In Aristotelian movement, as effective accomplishment, realized being-in-view of self, potential being actualized so that something of its incompletion remains in its actualization, Patočka finds in effect a mode of being suiting that of existence, insofar as the latter has to be what it is and therefore exists in the mode of its own accomplishment. Nevertheless, the Aristotelian theory of movement cannot be retained as such and so must be radicalized if we want to succeed in accounting for existence in its specificity. Indeed, change (which is the true term for movement) is a change that affects a foundation that, insofar as it is *what* changes, remains the same throughout the change. This is tantamount to saying that what is accomplished in the change is preceded in the foundation under the form of privation. Consequently change accomplishes a determination that was in a sense already in the foundation rather than producing it; it actualizes it rather than realizing it. Such is the limit of an assimilation of existential realization in Aristotelian movement. Although Aristotelian movement only leads something to its actuality, something that remains in a sense exterior to movement, by contrast the movement of existence creates what is itself in movement by this very movement; in other words, it realizes it. Aristotelian movement actualizes a possibility that was already present; the movement of existence creates possibility in realizing it. Patočka states this clearly:

Aristotelian movement is a change that takes place in the interval of contrary *givens*: a color can change only into another color, a sound into a sound, an inanimate substance into an animate substance and vice versa. The movement of existence is on the other hand the project of possibilities *as* their realization; they are not possibilities given in advance in a zone determining a "foundation." The "self" is not a foundation passively determined by the presence or the absence of a certain *eidos*, by a "figure" or a "privation"; it is something that determines itself and, in this sense, freely chooses its possibilities.[13]

This is why Patočka criticizes in a recurring way the maintenance in Aristotle of a basis for movement that keeps him from arriving at the true essence of mobility. We arrive at this essence only by means of a radicalization of the Aristotelian concept, a radicalization that requires that we abandon the notion of referring movement to an immutable foundation in order to conceive of it as what creates its own unity rather than receiving it from this foundation:

If, in place of this movement *belonging to something*, in place of possibilities that would be the property, the *having* of an identical something that is realized in them, we presuppose rather that this something *is* its possibility, that there is nothing in it *before* possibilities and *underlying* them, that it lives integrally only by the way in which it is in its possibilities—we will have then a *radicalization* of the Aristotelian concept of movement.[14]

We must therefore conceive of a movement that is not realization of something but that through which something occurs. This is why, to Patočka's way of thinking, the type of movement designated by the *genesis-phtora* (birth-death) pair, far from having a metaphorical meaning, must be thought of as what delivers the very essence of movement; it is the movement of substance, movement of emergence and of disappearing of the being that indicates the path toward the essence of movement. To say that a thing is *in* movement, is to say strictly that it *is* movement, in the sense that its being is not what precedes movement by being affected by it, but indeed is what movement realizes. Truly understood, movement does not unfold within the being. It does not lead from an already present being to a new determination of the same being; it is the process by which the being becomes what it is—in short, it leads the being to its being. Thus, to the Aristotelian concept that still unfolds at the level of the being, Patočka contrasts an *ontological* determination of movement. The latter is always ontogenic, meaning realization of what was not; otherwise it would no longer be movement but rather substitution of one determination by another. Movement must be understood as "original life that does not receive its unity from preserved foundation, but creates its own unity itself and that of the thing in movement. Only movement conceived of in this way is *original* movement."[15]

In this regard, we are confronted by a difficulty that we did not fully appreciate when writing *Le désir et la distance* and whose consideration leads us to nuance our second conclusion, in which we formulated the hypothesis of an originary movement, vis-à-vis which the very difference between movement of desire and that of manifestation would be derived. We have shown that it is due to a renewed concept of movement stemming from a meditation on Aristotelianism that Patočka succeeds in reconciling the existential difference between *Dasein* (upon which the possibility of perceptual intentionality depends) and its subsistence within a world, ultimately its flesh. Understood as realization, movement designates a deeper sense of being than the division among existentials and categories, a sense of being that therefore allows us to account for the essence of the living human person insofar as this division is mingled in it. But what is the precise significance of this concept of movement and of corporeality that is its correlative? What exactly is their extension? Must we understand it in a highly particular sense of a living movement radically different from the movements of beings that are not on the level of *Dasein*, but simply on the level of bodies? In this case, Patočka's approach would consist in giving a meaning to the incarnation of *Dasein* by recourse to a specific concept of movement, in other words deepening *Dasein's* ontico-ontological singularity by taking into consideration the conditions of its realization. Must we instead think of movement in a generic sense that would encompass the movement of existence as well as that of the stone that falls, which would justify the continuity, confirmed at least semantically, between my body and bodies?

In this case, it is indeed *Dasein's* singularity in relation to other beings that would be compromised, and with it the structure of correlation that characterizes phenomenological analysis, so that, by a sort of long detour coinciding with the return of transcendent subjectivity rendered unworldly toward the world, we would find ourselves in the prephenomenological situation of a human existence whose mode of being is not fundamentally distinguished from the world's other beings. Moreover, it seems in fact that this is the direction taken by Patočka. Far from being given exclusively as deepening of *Dasein's* specificity, the characterization of movement as realization appears rather as a way of arriving at the essence of all movement and what we can qualify as phenomenological dynamics as an introduction to cosmology.

The fragment of the book on Aristotle given as a note in the *Papiers phénoménologiques* edited by Abrams is revealing in this regard. Patočka points out that unquestionably Aristotle borrows his metaphysical concepts from the human world, and that his approach depends on anthropomorphism. Yet, we must still agree about the meaning of this anthropomorphism. Are the human structures identified by Aristotle projected on a nature that they would conceal or deform, or are they modalities of essential structures, vis-à-vis which they would constitute a privileged means of access?[16] Patočka responds unambiguously:

If anthropomorphism means a *subjectivism*, Aristotle's intention is quite the opposite. He does not intend to subjectivize the world, to "animate" it, and to "spiritualize" it. On the contrary, he attempts to discover *asubjective* structures, directly encompassing and explaining also, starting with the most universal principles, human phenomena, human understanding and behavior, things as characteristic of the human person as life in truth, the will and the act of deciding.[17]

We have to find a *common measure* between the world and the human person, to avoid the split produced by Platonism and Cartesianism—to understand the human person as a particular case of general ontological structures. Now, Patočka mentions precisely movement, "ontological movement" radically different from that of modern natural sciences, as a privileged example of structure allowing us to establish a bridge between the human and the extrahuman. Even if it involves an interpretation of Aristotle, there is no doubt that it is his own approach that Patočka is characterizing in this instance. The last sentences of the fragment just quoted allow no doubt to subsist: "Today, while philosophy looks again for an asubjective ontological foundation, a *dedogmatized* Aristotle is for this reason current."[18] Movement defined by Patočka as realization, thanks to a deepening of Aristotelian ontological movement, appears indeed as a general ontological structure capable of accounting for the movement of existence. Far from the latter being an exclusively human mode of being whose attribution to nature would stem from a subjective projection contravening the division of modes of being (such would ultimately be Heidegger's position), the movement of existence is only a case, undoubtedly eminent, of a general essence of movement as realization. What applies for the human person applies therefore also for what is not human, and it is because the movement of existence is eminently movement that it can constitute a way of privileged access to other movements.

Correlatively, my flesh is also a body, and it is by virtue of this that it can bring forth an illumination of other bodies. This is what Patočka suggests on several occasions. He wonders, in his *Papiers phénoménologiques*: "Perhaps originary movement is not *things'* change of *place*, but indeed rather this dynamic surge that carries existence outside itself, that means that it is always already outside of self, that it exceeded itself *in the direction of things*, that it became a *seeing force*."[19] Undoubtedly, the modern conception of movement is derived and abstract; hence it requires an ontological determination that is given within our own existence but that does not apply exclusively to it. As is the case in Aristotle, movement conceived of as realization is indeed, for Patočka, an asubjective structure able to encompass and explain human phenomena, in particular the essence of *Dasein*. The phenomenology of movement, grasped first directly from our existence, has unquestionably an ontological import.

The ontology of life can be broadened to include an ontology of the world if we understand life as movement in the original sense of the word—this movement that Aristotle was after with his concept of *realized dunamis*. If *dunamis* viewed as foundation, uprooted from spatio-temporality and forcibly reintegrated in the present-subsistent framework of substance, is deprived of a part of its ontological import, *human life as dunamis*, as possibility that is realized, is on the other hand in a position to restore to the concepts of space, time, and movement, their original ontological significance.[20]

But do we not restore in this way, in a certainly more elaborated form, the ontological naïveté against which all of phenomenology has been constructed? In effect, the latter, whether in Husserl or in Heidegger, aims at referring phenomenality (sense of being of being) to a particular being (consciousness or *Dasein*), whose mode of being cannot be that of worldly beings, whose manifestation it conditions. As Husserl affirms forcefully in *The Crisis of European Sciences and Transcendental Phenomenology*, phenomenology brings to the fore the correlation between the transcendent being and its subjective modes of given. This means that there is an irreducible *distance* or *tear*, constitutive of phenomenality, between appearing and the being on which its manifestations rest, so that the search for a univocal sense of being that would embrace the appearing being and the "locus" of constitution is not pertinent. The difficulty is rather to think of the difference of the being conditioning the manifestation in such a way that its "beingness," its intraworldliness, is not compromised by this difference.

It is indeed on this condition, which is not realized by Husserl, that the transcendence of what is constituted can be preserved; only a subject that is *of the* world can open itself *to the* world in the fullness of its meaning. It involves therefore conceiving simultaneously the ontological continuity of the human subject vis-à-vis the world and the ontological difference of level. As we have pointed out, if this is indeed what Heidegger is aiming at, it is uncertain whether he succeeds in accounting for (starting with *Dasein* itself) this continuity that is its intraworldliness. Moreover, this is unquestionably what Patočka's philosophy concerns itself with, on the basis of what we have called phenomenological dynamics.

But in characterizing *Dasein* by a movement in which the essence of all worldly movement becomes apparent, does not Patočka engage phenomenology on a path toward cosmological monism in which the singularity of *Dasein*'s mode of being (and consequently the very possibility of correlation) would be lost? It is true that this in no way involves a return to a naïve ontology that would base the continuity of the beings' sense of being on their substantiality. On the contrary, Patočka's theory of movement allows us to conceive of an intraworldliness that is not based on substantiality and that does not therefore compromise *Dasein*'s singularity. But everything occurs as if, in clarifying *Dasein*'s mode of being, in justifying fully its difference in relation to the *Vorhandenheit*, Patočka found himself forced to restore an ontological continuity on another level, a level discovered by means of the analysis of movement of a cosmology. Determining *Dasein*'s ultimate sense of being as movement of realization compromises its unicity at the very moment in which *its singularity* is fully revealed, as if a rigorous determination of the subject of the manifestation's sense of being had as its counterpart a questioning of the tear inherent in the correlation—as if, therefore, we abandoned phenomenology at the very moment in which we succeeded in establishing its possibility.

These, then, are the ultimate questions that I have invited my readers to consider: Is it possible (and on what conditions) to account for the difference between the appearing and the subject of manifestations on the basis of the monistic cosmology envisaged by this philosophy of movement? Does the concept of movement as realization allow us to maintain the originary difference between the movement of existence and the beings that it makes appear? How can the univocality of the ontologico-cosmological concept of movement be reconciled with the correlation and therefore with the difference of phenomenology's constitutive sense of being? In short, does the cosmological monism outlined by Patočka by means of an unprecedented deepening of the human subject's sense of being threaten the phenomenological undertaking, or does it constitute its most radical accomplishment?

REFERENCE MATTER

Notes

Translator's note: When English translations for works referred to in the text are available, we have used them in our translation. Minor changes may be made to fit these translations within our text. References to these translations are included in brackets following the references in the original text. Here is an alphabetical list of abbreviations for frequently cited texts (see the Bibliography for full information):

CE	*Creative Evolution* (Bergson)
Crisis	*The Crisis of European Sciences and Transcendental Phenomenology* (Husserl)
DG	*Der Gestaltkreis* (Von Weizsäcker)
DAO	*Der Aufbau des Organismus* (Goldstein)
EU	*Erfahrung und Urteil* (Husserl)
ID I	*Ideas Pertaining to a Pure Phenomenology and to a Phenomenological Philosophy, Book I* (Husserl)
IS	*The Incarnate Subject: Malebranche, Biran, and Bergson on the Union of Body and Soul* (Merleau-Ponty)
LI	*Logical Investigations* (Husserl)
MEH	*Le monde naturel et le mouvement de l'existence humaine* (Patočka)
MM	*Matter and Memory* (Bergson)
Nature	*La nature: Notes de cours du Collège de France* (Merleau-Ponty)
NC	*Notes de cours* (Merleau-Ponty)
PP	*Papiers phénoménologiques* (Patočka)
QQP	*Qu'est-ce que la phénomenologie?* (Patočka)
Sens	*Le Sens du temps et de la perception chez Husserl* (Granel)
VI	*The Visible and the Invisible* (Merleau-Ponty)
VSS	*Von Sinn der Sinne* (Straus)

INTRODUCTION: *The Problem of Perception*

1. M. Pradines, *La fonction perceptive* (Paris: Denoël-Gonthier, 1981), 27.

2. M. Merleau-Ponty, *Le visible et l'invisible* (Paris: Gallimard, 1964), 51; edited by C. Lefort and translated by A. Lingis under the title *The Visible and the Invisible* (Evanston, IL: Northwestern University Press, 1968), 30. Hereafter referred to as *VI*.

3. *VI*, 56 [34].

4. *Sens et non sens* (Paris: Nagel, 1948), 187; (reedited Paris: Gallimard, 1996), 114; translated by H. L. Dreyfus and P. Dreyfus under the title *Sense and Non-Sense* (Evanston, IL: Northwestern University Press, 1964), 93.

5. *VI*, 17 [3].

6. *Die Krisis der europaischen Wissenschaften und die transzendentale Phänomenologie* (Paris: Gallimard, 1976), 189; translated by G. Granel; English translation by D. Carr under the title *The Crisis of European Sciences and Transcendental Phenomenology* (Evanston, IL: Northwestern University Press, 1970), 159. Hereafter referred to as *Crisis*.

7. On this point, refer to my study *La perception—Essai sur le sensible* (Paris: Hatier, 1994).

8. Regarding this question, see Jacques Garelli's remarkable analysis in *Rythmes et mondes* (Grenoble: Millon, 1991), 124–38.

9. Husserl makes a certain number of modifications that are discussed at length in *Logical Investigations* but that do not interest us here; what is relevant here is how Husserl approaches perception.

10. *Logische Untersuchungen,* translated by H. Élie, A. L. Kelkel, and R. Schérer (Paris: PUF, 1993), II, 2, 172; English translation by J. N. Findlay under the title *Logical Investigations: Edmund Husserl* (London: Routledge and Kegan Paul; New York: Humanities Press, 2000), 556. Hereafter referred to as *LI*.

11. *LI*, II, 2, 234 [598].

12. *LI*, III, 69 [708–9].

13. *LI*, III, 98 [728–29].

14. *LI*, III, 98 [728].

15. *LI*, III, 85 [720].

16. *Ideen zu einer reinen Phänomenologie und phänomenologischen Philosophie I,* translated by P. Ricœur (Paris: Gallimard, 1950), 15; English translation by F. Kersten under the title *Edmund Husserl: Ideas Pertaining to a Pure Phenomenology and to a Phenomenological Philosophy,* Book I: *General Introduction to a Pure Phenomenology* (Boston: Martinus Nijhoff, 1983), 6. Hereafter referred to as *ID I*.

17. *ID I*, 78 [44].

18. *LI*, III, 175 [785].

19. See, for example, *ID I*, 126 [82].

20. *LI*, 74 [712].

21. We have consciously chosen "manifestations," more or less neutral, rather than the term *lived experience*, which Husserl uses and whose meaning we will have to discuss.

22. *ID I*, 132 [87].
23. *ID I*, 138 [91–92].
24. *ID I*, 137 [93].
25. *ID I*, 139 [95].

CHAPTER 1: *Critique of Transcendental Phenomenology*

1. *ID I*, 108 [63].
2. *ID I*, 122 [78].
3. *ID I*, 146 [99].
4. *ID I*, 148 [100].
5. *ID I*, 134 [88].
6. *ID I*, 134 [88].
7. See *ID I*, section 97 [236–40].
8. *ID I*, 289 [204].
9. *ID I*, 131 [86].
10. *VI*, 22 [7].
11. *VI*, 22 [7].
12. G. Granel, *Le sens du temps et de la perception chez Husserl* (Paris: Gallimard, 1968), 234. Hereafter referred to as *Sens*.
13. *ID I*, 131 [86].
14. *Sens*, 237.
15. *VI*, 22 [77].
16. We set aside for now the outline of the constitution of the *hylé* itself in originary temporality. In effect, the fact that the *hylé* is itself constituted—in other words, finally perceived through temporal "adumbrations" so that its test presupposes a sort of minimal distance that is nothing more than that of temporal passage—does not change anything in regard to the fact that it is distinguished, as constituted *hylé*, from the noesis that animates it and confers upon it the status of appearance of—in short, the fact that the analysis of perception remains entirely dependent on the model matter-form and the fact that the constitutive distance of appearance is ultimately completely ignored.
17. J. Patočka, *Qu'est-ce que la phénoménologie?*, translated by E. Abrams (Grenoble: Millon, 1988), 235. Hereafter referred to as *QQP*.
18. *QQP*, 235.
19. *QQP*, 207.
20. From this point of view, Michel Henry's perspective, which is the exact opposite of the one to which we ascribe, appears more consistent than ours in that at least it finally comes to recognize and thematize the dimension of absolute immanence without distance that is constitutive of lived experience and that Husserl does not want to assume completely. This is why Henry criticizes the submission of Husserlian thought regarding phenomenality to the order of distance or transcendence. In attempting to elaborate a theory of intentionality on the basis of the concept of lived experience, Husserl puts himself therefore in an awkward position

and finds himself criticized by the tenets of a theory of pure autoaffection as well as by those who judge that perceptual subjectivity must dispense with the concept of lived experience. Thus, in a sense Henry's philosophy appears as a more consistent theory of lived experience than Husserl's does. However, the real question, to our way of thinking, is to know if, phenomenologically, the concept of lived experience has a meaning.

21. See *QQP*, 208, 237, and *Papiers phénoménologiques*, translated by E. Abrams (Grenoble: Millon, 1995), 182. Hereafter referred to as *PP*.

22. *QQP*, 243.

23. *QQP*, 243. See also 203 and *PP*, 170, 176, 178, 255.

24. *QQP*, 239. Our emphasis.

25. *PP*, 178.

26. *QQP*, 203. See *PP*, 173: "*emptiness is in no way a non-givenness but a mode of given.*"

27. *ID I*, 142 [95].

28. *LI*, III, 74 [712].

29. *LI*, 75 [713].

30. *LI*, 85 [720].

31. *LI*, 86 [720].

32. See R. Bernet, *La vie du sujet* (Paris: PUF, 1994), 128: "We can say that in the contradictions of the *Logical Investigations* there is already outlined what will become the solution proposed by *Ideas I*. The failure of the *Logical Investigations* stems from the fact that their concept of the thing-in-itself of external perception contradicts the necessity of a partial or perspectivist given of the spatial thing."

33. *Sens*, 228, 241.

34. *ID I*, 478 [341].

35. *ID I*, 481 [343].

CHAPTER 2: *Phenomenological Reduction as Critique of Nothingness*

1. Patočka defines "the original intention of phenomenology" in this manner: "to introduce to the apparent not the *appearing*, but the *appearance*, the appearance of the appearing, that itself does not appear in the manifestation of the latter." *PP*, 196.

2. *VI*, 147 [109].

3. *VI*, 149 [111].

4. *VI*, 149 [111].

5. *VI*, 214–15 [162]. Our emphasis.

6. On this point see G. Deleuze, *Le bergsonisme* (Paris: PUF, 1966).

7. H. Bergson, *L'évolution créatrice*, Edition du Centenaire (Paris: PUF, 1959), 728; translated by A. Mitchell as *Creative Evolution* (New York: Holt, 1911), 275. Hereafter referred to as *CE*.

8. *CE*, 728 [276].

9. *CE*, 729 [276].

10. *CE*, 747 [298]

11. *CE*, 302 [248]. Bergson also considers this attitude as inevitable, as we see later, but for somewhat different reasons.

12. *CE*, 743 [294].

13. In a sense of essence, this cannot be that which we have criticized because it would be absolutely contradictory to bring to essence in the Husserlian sense experience's inability to take, vis-à-vis the real, the field that is precisely necessary for the grasping of an essence.

14. *CE*, 283 [283].

15. It is striking to observe that Husserl himself, in section 21 of *Erfahrung und Urteil* (translated by D. Souche, Paris: PUF, 1970, 103; hereafter referred to as *EU*), develops a theory of the "origin of negation" that in many respects is close to Bergson's. In effect, negation is not only a question of predicative judgment but also rooted originarily in the antepredicative sphere. It consists precisely in the experience of a deception, of the suppression of an anticipatory intention by an impression that conflicts with what was expected.

16. *CE*, 745 [296].

17. See B. Prado, *Presença e campo transcendental: Consciência e negatividade na filosofia de Bergson* (São Paulo: Editora da Universidade de São Paulo, 1988), 56.

18. *CE*, 746 [297].

19. H. Bergson, *Matière et mémoire* (Paris: PUF, 1959), 321; translated by N. M. Paul and W. S. Palmer under the title *Matter and Memory* (London: Allen & Unwin, 1950), 241. Hereafter referred to as *MM*.

20. M. Merleau-Ponty, *Notes de cours, 1959–1961* (Paris: Gallimard, 1996), 84. Our emphasis. Hereafter referred to as *NC*.

21. See *MM*, chap. 3, and G. Deleuze, *Différence et répétition* (Paris: PUF, 1968), 108–16.

22. *ID I*, 151 [102–3].

23. *Sens*, 244.

24. For a precise discussion and critique of this important passage, see Patočka, *Introduction à la phénoménologie de Husserl* (Grenoble: Millon, 1992), 138–41.

25. *VI*, 225 [171–72].

26. *NC*, 360. He evokes also reduction in these terms, in an unpublished text dating from June 1959: "We admit a sort of 'reduction': not a reduction to *meaning* (from whence, by overturning, system of *Sinngebung*) but reduction to the prepersonal and meta-personal *Weltthesis*, to the 'there is' . . . there is no *nothing*, to the *Offenheit* as structure of Being, word of Being."

27. On this question, see Merleau-Ponty, "Le philosophe et son ombre," in *Signes* (Paris: Gallimard, 1960); translated with an introduction by R. C. McCleary under the title *Signs* (Evanston, IL: Northwestern University Press, 1964).

28. *Crisis*, 161 [142].

CHAPTER 3: *The Three Moments of Appearance*

1. *PP*, 114.

2. *PP*, 214. Our emphasis.

3. *PP*, 222.

4. Thus we can understand why Merleau-Ponty never abandons the reference to the psychology of form and attempts in his working notes for *The Visible and The Invisible* to give to the figure-ground structure an ontological scope that it obviously does not have in *The Structure of Behavior*. For example, *VI*, 245 [191]: "To be conscious—to have a figure on a ground—one cannot go back any further" and 246 [192]: "figure on a ground, the simplest '*Etwas*'—the *Gestalt* contains the key to the problem of the mind."

5. *PP*, 260.

6. Merleau-Ponty is unquestionably the first to have clearly understood this, as *Phenomenology of Perception* confirms, in particular the chapter devoted to the *cogito*. Instead of approaching perception on the basis of consciousness, he approaches consciousness that is based on perception, essentially perception of a world. This signifies not only that consciousness is a moment of perception but also that consciousness of self is a perception.

7. *PP*, 197, 255.

8. *VI*, 304 [250–51].

9. *PP*, 127, 171.

10. It is this double envelopment that Merleau-Ponty has in mind in the concepts of chiasma and flesh.

11. It seems to us, despite a clear vision of the characteristic structure of appearance that he thematizes in terms of chiasma and differential unity of the visible and the invisible, Merleau-Ponty does not pose with sufficient clarity the question of the sense of being of the perceiving subject. Although he recognizes the essential inscription of the seeing subject in the visible, he continues to determine the former on the level of lived experiences. He attempts to arrive at the specificity of the carnal body on the basis of the "touching-touched" and by presupposing thus the dimension of lived experience—even if it is in order to question it by demonstrating the impossibility of coincidence. He does not consider the sense of being of the "subjective" in abandoning purely and simply the order of lived experience—in other words, in asking what the mode of existing is of this being that grasps the visible as presentation of an invisible. The persistence of a form of subjectivism inherited from Husserl and evident until Merleau-Ponty's last work undoubtedly explains the difficulties reflected in writing *The Visible and the Invisible*.

12. Such is precisely Sartre's attitude. He attempts to reconstitute phenomenality from the duality between being in self and a purely negative nothingness, instead of accepting the immediate identity between the negative and the positive, in other words from the characteristic figure of phenomenality. The dialectic, in the Sartrian sense, appears then as an attempt to rejoin this phenomenality. It is a hopeless attempt since we cannot rejoin an immediate identity, or rather the immediate

as identity between being and nothingness, through the interplay that their duality allows.

13. It is obvious that these propositions call for a confrontation with Heidegger on the question of nothingness. Merleau-Ponty outlines this in the 1958–59 course notes, 101–4. This confrontation brings into play the difficult question of the status of nothingness in Heidegger's work. We will reserve that for a future study.

14. Concerning which we ask in any case how a phenomenology of duration can dispense with it.

15. G. Lebrun, *La patience du concept* (Paris: Gallimard, 1972), 240.

16. See Merleau-Ponty in *VI* (Annex), 211 [159]: "We are interrogating our experience precisely in order to know how it opens us to what is not ourselves. This does not even exclude the possibility that we find in our experience a movement toward what could not in any event be present to us in the original and whose irremediable absence would thus count among our originating experiences."

17. See *PP*, 176: "The world is originarily given, but *everything* is not given in the same way. Originarity is not a unitarian mark, it involves on the contrary gradations and diverse qualities. Thus, what is given as qualitatively present is originarily given in another sense than what, in connection with the same being, is given as empty, in a non-qualitative way; emptiness is in no way a non-givenness, but a *mode of given*."

18. *PP*, 178.

19. *PP*, 246.

20. *PP*, 217.

21. *VI*, 195 [148–49]. Translator's note: we have changed Lingis's translation from "things held" (*chose tenues*) to "slender things" (*chose ténues*) as it appears in the original French text.

22. We point out that Husserl is often quite close to recognizing the constitutive dimension of horizon and that it is his intuitionist conception, and ultimately empiricist conception of presence, that keeps him from accepting all that follows. This hesitation is obvious, for example, in *EU*, section 8.

23. Merleau-Ponty defines transcendence as "identity within difference" (*VI*, 279 [225]).

24. *VI*, 300 [247].

25. *VI*, 207, [214]. In a sense, our entire undertaking consists in trying to justify and understand this affirmation.

CHAPTER 4: *Perception and Living Movement*

1. See *PP*, 204. It is this situation that Merleau-Ponty attempts to describe in terms of chiasma or intertwining between my body and the world. The body envelops the world, that is to say makes it appear, only to the degree to which it is enveloped by it, so that the manifestation of the world *for* the body is at the same time manifestation of the world *by itself* within the body, so that the body's constituting power coincides with the phenomenalizing potency of the world. This intertwining

reveals therefore an ontological continuity between the body and the world, a co-belonging deeper than their opposition; and it is this cobelonging that the concept of Flesh receives. Flesh designates nothing more than the element itself of appearance insofar as it has, as constitutive moments, the appearing world and a subject that is on this side of what it makes appear, and is consequently incarnated.

2. *VI*, 304 [205].

3. Such was in a way the perspective of *The Structure of Behavior*, written at a time when Merleau-Ponty was still not too familiar with Husserl. With *Phenomenology of Perception*, he passes to an "internal" point of view that he henceforth does not abandon. The phenomenon of belonging is approached then principally on the basis of the test of incarnation as it is affirmed in the self-touching. Thus, the late texts, inspired by Husserl's *Ideen II*, represent in a way a step back in regard to the question of the subject's nature face vis-à-vis the first work. Nevertheless, we must set aside the lecture series on *La Nature*, which represents Merleau-Ponty's most advanced reflection concerning the living subject.

4. J. Derrida, *La voix et le phénomène* (Paris: PUF, 1967), 14; translated by D. B. Allison and N. Garver under the title *Speech and Phenomena and Other Essays on Husserl's Theory of Signs* (Evanston, IL: Northwestern University Press, 1973), 14–15.

5. K. Goldstein, *Der Aufbau des Organismus*, translation by Burckhardt and Kuntz (Paris: Gallimard, 1951), 223. Hereafter referred to as *DAO*.

6. V. von Weizsäcker, *Der Gestaltkreis*, translated by M. Foucault (Bruges, Desclée De Brouwer, 1958), 156. Hereafter referred to as *DG*.

7. *DG*, 197.

8. We should show here that there is an originary sense of the grasp that is deeper than the distinction between manual prehension and intellectual apprehension and that gives them meaning. Thus it would not be metaphorically that I can claim to have grasped an idea. As Minkowski suggests, attention represents perhaps the originary meaning of grasp; it is at the suture between intellectual apprehension and physical movement and thus bears its double possibility.

9. E. Minkowski, *Vers une cosmologie* (Paris: Aubier-Montaigne, 1936), 91.

10. Minkowski shows that attention, far from being an immobile fixation, implies a multitude of internal movements of relaxation of vigilance, of inattention.

11. M. Merleau-Ponty, *L'œil et l'esprit* (Paris: NRF, 1964), 17; translated by C. Doller as "Eye and Mind," in *The Primacy of Perception* (Evanston, IL: Northwestern University Press, 1964), 162. See also *DG*, 15: "We do not know if it is sensation that guides movement, or if it is movement that determines the place and the how of each sensation. Because movement, like a sculptor, creates the object, and sensation receives it as in an ecstasy."

12. *PP*, 66.

13. *PP*, 73.

14. It is obvious that such a conclusion would call for confronting Maine de Biran's philosophy. According to him, in effect the self is constituted as such only in effort, in the test of a resistance that is first that of the body itself. The self and

the resisting pole are related since they emerge from the very unfolding of effort. It is in manifesting itself effectively that effort meets a resisting pole and is constituted therefore as effort of a self.

15. M. Merleau-Ponty, *La nature: Notes de cours du Collège de France* (Paris: Seuil, 1995), 273. Hereafter referred to as *Nature*.

16. *Nature*, 284.

17. *MM*, 183 [23].

18. *MM*, 185 [27].

19. This naturally echoes Merleau-Ponty's assertion according to which "I am sure that there is being, on condition of not looking for another sort of being than being for me." It is therefore not surprising that Merleau-Ponty became interested very early in the Bergsonian theory of images, as confirms for example his 1936 review of Sartre's *L'imagination*. It would undoubtedly not be an exaggeration to say that Merleau-Ponty concerned himself, throughout his work, with giving a satisfying ontological status to this concept of image.

20. M. Merleau-Ponty, *L'union de l'âme et du corps chez Malebranche, Biran et Bergson*, notes recueillies par J. Deprun (Paris: Vrin, 1978), 81; translated by P. Milan under the title *The Incarnate Subject: Malebranche, Biran, and Bergson on the Union of Body and Soul* (Amherst, NY: Humanity Books, 2001) 89. Hereafter referred to as *IS*.

21. *IS*, 81 [89].

22. *IS*, 87 [94].

CHAPTER 5: *Desire as Essence of Subjectivity*

1. *PP*, 19.

2. "Intuition et re-présentation, intuition et remplissement" (1893) and "Appendices aux *Études psychologiques pour la logique élémentaire*" (1893), in Husserl-Twardowski, *Sur les objets intentionnels* (1893–1901), translated by J. English (Paris: Vrin, 1993). Regarding this question, see B. Bégout, "Problèmes d'une phénoménologie de la sexualité: Intentionnalité pulsionnelle et pulsion sexuelle chez Husserl," in *Phénoménologie et psychanalyse*, under the direction of J. C. Beaune (Seyssel, France: Champ Vallon, 1998).

3. *Autrement qu'être ou au-delà de l'essence* (La Haye: Nijhoff, 1978), 83; translated by A. Lingis under the title of *Otherwise than Being or Beyond Essence* (Boston: Martinus Nijhoff, 1981), 66.

4. In the final analysis, our view of horizon leads us to the same conclusion. Because manifestation relies on a nucleus of sensible presence and therefore on a current consciousness, horizon can, in Husserl, refer only to a potentiality of consciousness. On the contrary, in confusing the difference between emptiness and fulfillment and in therefore putting horizon at the heart of appearance, we are led to conceive of consciousness *as potentiality*. Inasmuch as the subject is subject for the horizon, it can exist only in the mode of tension, of difference from self—in other words, of desire.

5. *Husserliana, XIV*, 334. Quoted by Bégout, in the article "Problèmes" (note 2 of this chapter), upon which we rely for what concerns this precise point, 52.

6. Manuscrit C16/40a et 36a, translated by A. Montavont. These references are taken from her thesis "De la phénoménologie génétique: passivité, vie et affection chez Husserl," which appeared under the title *De la passivité chez Husserl* (Paris: PUF, 1999). Hereafter referred to as Montavont.

7. Montavont, 507.

8. Montavont, 549.

9. Montavont, 509–15, 560, and following.

10. Even if it developed principally in Germany, this tradition has unquestionably had echoes in France. Canguilhem's epistemological thought is deeply inspired by Goldstein's. In the field of biology, strictly speaking, André Pichot's works, based on contemporary biological research, lead to conclusions close to those that we are attempting to elaborate here. We mention in particular the *Éléments pour une théorie de la biologie* (Paris: Maloine, 1980) and *Petite phénoménologie de la connaissance* (Paris: Aubier, 1991). Also, *L'individu et sa genèse physico-biologique* by G. Simondon (Grenoble: Millon, 1995) represents a reference text for any phenomenological approach to the living subject.

11. *DAO*, 95. See also *DG*, 208: "The unity of the subject is constituted only in its untiring restoration beyond variations and crises."

12. *DAO*, 269.

13. E. Straus, *Von Sinn Der Sinne*, translated by G. Thinès et J.-P. Legrand (Grenoble: Millon, 1989), 46. Hereafter referred to as VSS.

14. *DAO*, 440 (see also 401).

15. *DAO*, 402, 443. We find a comparable idea in Minkowski, under the term of anthropocosmic conflict. See *Vers une cosmologie*, 196–98.

16. As Patočka writes, "The living of experience is like a weft stretched between two horizons: one is my self, the other the world. Living is a way of clarifying these horizons, having the feature that, in order to explain myself, I must first be grounded in the world" (*PP*, 63).

17. *VSS*, 390. See also *VSS*, 396, 573.

18. *VSS*, 398.

19. *DG*, 143.

20. "It is not the physiological functions of sensory organs that make a being a sensing being, but rather this possibility of approaching, and the latter belongs neither to perception by itself, nor to movement by itself" (*VSS*, 378).

21. See *VSS*, 617: "Distance is therefore relative to a being in becoming and animated by desire; it is the scope of its grasp that determines the articulation of the distance in the near and the far." We must, however, recognize that we have here the only explicit mention of desire in this work, even if desire is implied by the relation of totality. This perspective must of course be compared with Heidegger's, who shows that perception requires the opening of a preliminary distance that gives the very sense of subsistence (see M. Heidegger, *Die Grundprobleme der*

Phänomenologie, translated by J. F. Courtine, Paris: NRF, 1985, 96–98. But we must add, in diametrical opposition to what Heidegger claims, that this distance is none other than that of the world, which hides in each manifestation; it is therefore correlative of a living subject.

CONCLUSION

1. *PP*, 177.

2. This is why what is true for time is not true for duration. In effect, insofar as it confirms an interiority that does not form an alternative with heterogeneity and manifests a form of permanence in passage, Bergsonian duration was destined to acquire an ontological significance and no longer just a psychological significance.

3. *PP*, 157.

4. *PP*, 157.

5. P. Ricœur, *Le volontaire et l'involontaire* (Paris: Aubier, 1950), I, 397; translated, with an introduction by E. V. Kohák under the title *Freedom and Nature: The Voluntary and the Involuntary* (Evanston, IL: Northwestern University Press, 1966), 423.

6. *VI*, 318, 321 [265, 268].

7. *PP*, 108.

8. This is the reason it appears to us more and more legitimate to organize a confrontation between a certain phenomenological current and Bergson's thought, in particular in *Creative Evolution*. Such research would eventually demonstrate the inscription of French phenomenology in a tradition summarily qualified as spiritualist, a tradition that runs from Maine de Biran to Merleau-Ponty, passing through Bergson and Ravaisson.

9. In this regard, it would be possible to clearly distinguish two traditions. One, which goes from Heidegger and Straus to Maldiney, tends to emphasize separation; the other, which goes from Husserl and Von Weizsäcker to Merleau-Ponty, places the accent more on continuity.

10. *VSS*, 319.

11. H. Maldiney, *Penser l'homme et la folie* (Grenoble: Millon, 1991), 385.

12. This is, to our way of thinking, Heidegger's philosophical attitude, at least in *Sein und Zeit*. The characterization of *Dasein* by anxiety, opening upon nothingness from which a being can be given, is correlative with a fundamental lack of comprehension of the true meaning of flesh, in other words of desire.

13. *Nature*, 207.

14. *VSS*, 428.

AUTHOR'S AFTERWORD

1. See Heidegger's *Lettre à Husserl du 22 octobre 1927, Annexe 1*, translated by J. F. Courtine (Paris: Editions de l'Herne, 1983), 83.

2. J. Patočka, *Le monde naturel et le mouvement de l'existence humaine*, translated by E. Abrams (Dordrecht: Kluwer, 1988), 255. Hereafter referred to as *MEH*.

3. M. Heidegger, *Die Grundprobleme der Phänomenologie.* Translated by J. F. Courtine. Paris: Gallimard, 1985, 200. See also *MEH,* 102.

4. In a letter to Robert Campbell dated May 12, 1914, Patočka refers to his reading of *Le visible et l'invisible* and to its contribution concerning the question of the subject-object relationship. Moreover, he adds, "these are things that Heidegger neglected in *Sein und Zeit* in which he omits incarnation in *Dasein*'s structure. . . . One day, we will have to integrate them in *Dasein*'s total structure, which Merleau himself was unable to achieve."

5. *MEH,* 93.

6. *MEH,* 96.

7. Life loses its problematic status once it is accessible "privatively" starting with *Dasein* while blurring the separation between existence and *Vorhandenheit.*

8. *MEH,* 105. This certainly does not exclude the fact that we must distinguish between existence and life. We must introduce differences within the movement of existence. See, for example *MEH,* 105.

9. *PP,* 107. See also *MEH,* 102.

10. *VI,* 51 [30]. We must point out here, to be accurate, that Merleau-Ponty thematized this motor determination of the body. See *Le visible et l'invisible,* 277 [229], 284 [234], 302 [248], 310 [254], 313 [259].

11. *PP,* 107; *MEH,* 102.

12. *MEH,* 250.

13. *MEH,* 263.

14. *PP,* 107; *MEH,* 103.

15. *MEH,* 103.

16. In this instance, Patočka's reading of Aristotle arrives at the same conclusion as Hans Jonas, who in *The Phenomenon of Life* (New York: HarperCollins, 1966, 23) challenges the rejection of anthropomorphism and sets forth a positive anthropomorphism that discovers in the human person a privileged access to being: "Perhaps rightly understood, man *is* after all the measure of all things—not indeed through the legislation of his reason but through the exemplar of his psychophysical totality which represents the maximum of concrete ontological completeness known to us."

17. *PP,* 30.

18. *PP,* 31.

19. *PP,* 72.

20. *MEH,* 102.

Bibliography

Translator's note: The items that appear with an asterisk have been added by the author to the Bibliography created for this English translation.

Badiou, A. *Deleuze "La clameur de l'Etre."* Paris: Hachette, 1997.

Bégout, B. "Problèmes d'une phénoménologie de la sexualité. Intentionalité pulsionnelle et pulsion sexuelle chez Husserl." In *Phénoménologie et psychanalyse*, under the direction of J. C. Beaune. Seyssel, France: Champ Vallon, 1998.

Bergson, H. *Œuvres*, Édition du centenaire. Paris: PUF, 1959.

Bernet, R. *La vie du sujet. Recherches sur l'interprétation de Husserl dans la phénoménologie.* Paris: PUF, 1994.

Brisart, R. "La reduction et l'irréductible phénoménologique. Husserl critique de Heidegger." In *L'évidence du monde. Méthode et empirie de la phénoménologie*, under the direction of R. Brisart and R. Célis. Brussels Facultés Universitaires Saint-Louis, 1994.

Buytenduijk, F.J.J. *Traité de psychologie animale.* Trans. A. Franck-Duquesne. Paris: PUF, 1952.

Canguilhem, G. *La connaissance de la vie.* Paris: Vrin, 1965.

——. *Le normal et le pathologique.* Paris: PUF, 1966.

Célis, R. "*L'Urdoxa* dans la vie intentionnelle." In *L'évidence du monde. Méthode et empirie de la phénoménologie*, under the direction of R. Brisart et R. Célis. Brussels Facultés Universitaires de Saint-Louis, 1994.

Chambon, R. *Le monde comme perception et réalité.* Paris: Vrin, 1974.

Courtine, J.-F. *Heidegger et la phénoménologie.* Paris: Vrin, 1990.

Dastur, F. "Pour une zoologie privative." *ALTER*, 1995, no. 3.

——. "Pour une phénoménologie de l'événement: l'attente et la surprise." *Etudes phénoménologiques*, 1997, no. 25.

——. "Eugen Fink—Mondanéité et mortalité." In N. Depraz and M. Richir (eds.), *Eugen Fink—Actes du Colloque de Cerisy-la-Salle 23–30 Juillet, 1994.* Amsterdam/Atlanta, GA: Elementa, 1998.

Deleuze, G. *Le bergsonisme.* Paris: PUF, 1966.

——. *Différence et répétition.* Paris: PUF, 1968.

Depraz, N. "Temporalité et affection dans les manuscrits tardifs sur la temporalité (1929–1935) de Husserl." In *Temporalité et affection*, ALTER, 1994, no. 2.

Derrida, J. *La voix et le phénomène*. Paris: PUF, 1967.

*———. *De l'esprit—Heidegger et la question*. Paris: Galilee, 1987.

Fink, E. *Spiel als Weltsymbol*. Trans. H. Hildenbrand and A. Lindenber. Paris: Editions de Minuit, 1966.

———. *Proximité et distance*. Trans. J. Kessler. Grenoble: Millon, 1994.

*Frogneux, N. *Hans Jonas ou la vie dans le monde*. Paris: De Boeck, 2001.

Gadamer, H.-G. *Wahrheit und Methode*. Trans. P. Fruchon. Paris: Seuil, 1996.

Garelli, J. *Rythmes et mondes*. Grenoble: Millon, 1991.

Gennart, M. "Une phénoménologie des données hylétiques est-elle possible?" In *Les Enjeux de la psychologie phénoménologique, Études phénoménologiques*, 1986, no. 4.

Goldstein, K. *Der Aufbau des Organismus*. Trans. E. Burckhardt and J. Kunz. Paris: Gallimard, 1983.

Granel, G. *Le sens du temps et de la perception chez Husserl*. Paris: Gallimard, 1968.

Heidegger, M. *Der Satz vom Grund*. Trans. A. Préau. Paris: Gallimard, 1962.

———. *Was ist Metaphysik?* Trans. H. Corbin, R. Munier, in *Questions I*. Paris: Gallimard, 1968.

*———. "Lettre à Husserl du 22 octobre 1927." In *Heidegger*. Annexe 1. Trans. J. F. Courtine. Paris: Editions de l'Herne, 1983.

*———. *Die Grundprobleme der Phänomenologie*. Trans. J. F. Courtine. Paris: Gallimard, 1985.

———. *Sein und Zeit*. Trans. E. Martineau. Paris: Authentica, 1985.

*———. *Die Grundbegriffe der Metaphysik. Welt-Endlichkeit-Einsamkeit*. Francfort-sur-le-Main: Vittorio Klostermann, 1983. Trans. D. Panis. *Les concepts fondamentaux de la métaphysique. Monde-Finitude-Solitude*. Paris: Gallimard, 1992.

Henry, M. *L'essence de la manifestation*. Paris: PUF, 1963.

———. *Philosophie et phénoménologie du corps*. Paris: PUF, 1965.

Husserl, E. *Logische Untersuchungen*. Trans. H. Elie, A. L. Kelkel, and R. Schérer. Paris: PUF, 1959, 1961, 1963.

———. *Ding und Raum, Vorlesungen 1907*. Trans. J. F. Lavigne. Paris: PUF, 1989.

———. *Ideen zu einer reinen Phänomenologie und phänomenologischen Philosophie 1*. Halbband [*Ideas Pertaining to a Pure Phenomenology and to a Phenomenological Philosophy, Book I*]. Trans. P. Ricœur. Paris: Gallimard, 1950.

———. *Ideen . . . 2. Halbband*. Trans. E. Escoubas. Paris: PUF, 1982.

———. *Vorlesungen zur Phänomenologie des inneren Zeitbewußtsein*. Trans. H. Dussort. Paris: PUF, 1964.

———. *Cartesianische Meditationen*. Trans. G. Peiffer et E. Lévinas. Paris: Vrin, 1969.

———. *Die Krisis der europäischen Wissenschaften und die tranzendentale Phänomenologie*. Trans. G. Granel. Paris: Gallimard, 1976.

———. *Erfahrung und Urteil—Untersuchungen zur Genealogie der Logik*. Trans. D. Souche. Paris: PUF, 1970.

———. "Umsturz der kopernikanischen Lehre: die Erde als Ur-Arche bewegt sich nicht." Trans. D. Franck. *Philosophie*, 1984, no. 1.

———. *Universale Teleologie.* Trans. J. Benoist. Philosophie, 1989, no. 21.

Husserl, E., and Twardowski, K. *Sur les objets intentionnels.* Trans. J. English. Paris: Vrin, 1993.

Jankélévitch, V. *Bergson.* Paris: Alcan, 1931.

Jeannerod, M. *Le cerveau-machine.* Paris: Fayard, 1983.

Johnson, M. *The Body in the Mind.* Chicago: University of Chicago Press, 1987.

*Jonas, H. *Philosophische Untersuchungen und metaphysisch Vermutungen.* Insel Verlag, 1992; trans. S. Cornille and P. Ivernel. *Evolution et liberté.* Paris: Bibliothèque Rivages, 2000.

*———. *The Phenomenon of Life: Toward a Philosophical Biology.* New York: HarperCollins, 1966; trans. D. Loreis. *Le phénomène de la vie.* Paris: De Boeck, 2001.

*Lacan, J. *Le seminaire II—Le moi dans la théorie de Freud et dans la technique de la psychanalyse.* Paris: Seuil, 1978.

Lebrun, G. *La patience du concept.* Paris: Gallimard, 1972.

Lévinas, E. *La théorie de l'intuition dans la phénoménologie de Husserl.* Paris: Vrin, 1930.

———. *En découvrant l'existence avec Husserl et Heidegger.* Paris: Vrin, 1949.

———. *Totalité et infini—Essai sur l'extériorité.* Leiden: Nijhoff, 1961.

———. *Autrement qu'être ou au-delà de l'essence.* Leiden: Nijhoff, 1974.

Madinier, G. *Conscience et mouvement.* Paris: Alcan, 1938.

Maine De Biran, M.-F. *Mémoire sur la decomposition de la pensée.* Œuvres, ed. F. Azouvi. T. III. Paris: Vrin, 1988.

Maldiney, H. *Regard Parole Espace.* Lausanne: L'Age d'Homme, 1973.

———. *Penser l'homme et la folie.* Grenoble: Millon, 1991.

Malherbe, M. *Trois essais sur le sensible.* Paris: Vrin, 1991, 1998.

Merleau-Ponty, M. *La structure du comportement.* Paris: PUF, 1942.

———. *Phénoménologie de la perception.* Paris: Gallimard, 1945.

———. *Sens et non-sens.* Paris: Nagel, 1948.

———. *Signes.* Paris: Gallimard, 1960.

———. *L'œil et l'esprit.* Paris: Gallimard, 1964.

———. *Le visible et l'invisible.* Paris: Gallimard, 1964.

———. *Résumés de cours.* Collège de France 1952–1960. Paris: Gallimard, 1968.

———. *L'union de l'âme et du corps chez Malebranche, Biran et Bergson.* Paris: Vrin, 1968.

———. *La nature.* Paris: Seuil, 1995.

———. *Notes de cours* 1959–1961. Paris: Gallimard, 1996.

Minkowski, E. *Vers une cosmologie.* Paris: Aubier, 1967.

———. *Le temps vécu.* Paris: PUF, 1995.

*Montavont, A. *De la passivité chez Husserl.* Paris: PUF, 1999.

Montebello, P. *La decomposition de la pensée.* Grenoble: Millon, 1994.

Paci, E. "Commento al manoscritto E III 5." In *Tempo e intenzionalità*. Archivio di Filosofia, 1960.

———. "Per una fenomenologia dell'eros." *Aut-Aut*, 1961.

Pachoud, B. "The Teleological Dimension of Perceptual and Motor Intentionality." In J. Petitot, F. Varela, B. Pachoud and J.M. Roy (eds.), *Naturalizing Phenomenology*. Palo Alto, CA: Stanford University Press, 1999.

Patočka, J. *Le Monde naturel comme problème philosophique*. Trans. J. Danek and H. Declève. Leiden: Nijhoff, 1976.

———. *Le Monde naturel et le mouvement de l'existence humaine*. Trans. H. Declève. Leiden: Nijhoff, 1988.

———. *Qu'est-ce que la phénoménologie?* Trans. E. Abrams. Grenoble: Millon, 1988.

———. *Introduction à la phénoménologie de Husserl*. Trans. E. Abrams. Grenoble: Millon, 1992.

———. *Papiers phénoménologiques*. Trans. E. Abrams. Grenoble: Millon, 1995.

Pichot, A. *Éléments pour une théorie de la biologie*. Paris: Maloine, 1980.

———. *Petite phénoménologie de la connaissance*. Paris: Aubier, 1991.

Pradines, M. *Philosophie de la sensation*. Paris: Les Belles Lettres, 1928, 1932, 1934.

———. *La fonction perceptive*. Paris: Denoël-Gonthier, 1981.

Prado, B. *Presença e campo transcendental—Consciência e negatividade na filosofia de Bergson*. Editora da universidade de Sao Paulo, 1989.

Ravaisson, F. *De l'habitude*. Presentation par J.-F. Courtine. Paris: Vrin, 1984.

Ricœur, P. *Le volontaire et l' involontaire*. Paris: Aubier, 1950.

———. *De l'interprétation*. Paris: Seuil, 1965.

———. *A l'école de la phénoménologie*. Paris: Vrin, 1986.

Rodrigo, P. *Aristote—L' eidétique et la phénoménologie*. Grenoble: Millon, 1995.

Romano, C. "L'unité de l'espace et la phénoménologie." *Cahiers philosophiques de Strasbourg*, 1994, no. 1.

Rouger, F. *Existence-Monde-Origine, Essai sur le sens d'être de la finitude*. Paris: L'Harmattan, 1996.

———. *L'Evénement de monde, Essai sur les conditions pures de la phénoménalité*. Paris: L'Harmattan, 1997.

Ruyer, R. *La conscience et le corps*. Paris: Alcan, 1937.

———. *Néo-finalisme*. Paris: PUF, 1952.

Simondon, G. *L'individuation psychique et collective*. Paris: Aubier, 1989.

———. *L'individu et sa genèse physico-biologique*. Grenoble: Millon, 1995.

Scheler, M. *Die Stellung des Menschen im Kosmos*. Trans. M. Dupuy. Paris: Aubier, 1951.

Straus, E. *Vom Sinn der Sinne*. Trans. G. Thinès et J.-P. Legrand. Grenoble: Millon, 1989.

———. "Les formes du spatial." Trans. M. Gennart. In J. F. Courtine (ed.), *Figures de la subjectivité*. Paris: Éditions du C.N.R.S., 1992.

*Tinland, F. *La Différence anthropologique. Essai sur les rapports de la nature et de l' artifice*. Paris: Aubier Montaigne, 1977.

Valéry, P. "Théorie poétique et esthétique." In *Œuvres* T. 1. Paris: Gallimard, 1957.

Varela, F., Thompson, E., and Rosch, E. *L'Inscription corporelle de l'esprit*. Paris: Seuil, 1993.

——. *Quel savoir pour l'éthique?* Paris: Éditions la Découverte, 1996.

Villela, M. "L'Expérience anté-prédicative." In J. F. Courtine (ed.), *Phénoménologie et logique*. Paris: Presses de l'École Normale Supérieure, 1996.

Von Uexküll, J. *Streifzüge durch die Umwelten von Tieren und Menschen—Ein Bilderbuch unsichtbarer Welten*. Trans. Ph. Muller as *Mondes animaux et monde humain*. Paris: Denoël Médiations, 1965.

Von Weizsäcker, V. *Der Gestaltkreis*. Trans. M. Foucault. Paris: Desclée de Brouwer, 1958.

Whitehead, A. N. *Science and the Modern World*. Trans. P. Couturiau. Monaco: Editions du Rocher, 1994.

——. *Process and Reality*. Trans. D. Charles and others. Paris: Gallimard, 1995.

——. *The Concept of Nature*. Trans. J. Douchement. Paris: Vrin, 1998.

Worms, F. *Introduction à Matière et Mémoire de Bergson*. Paris: PUF, 1997.

*——. *Bergson et les deux sens de la vie*. Paris: PUF, Quadrige (forthcoming).

Index of Names

Brett Levinson, *The Ends of Literature: The Latin American 'Boom" in the Neoliberal Marketplace*

Timothy J. Reiss, *Against Autonomy: Cultural Instruments, Mutualities, and the Fictive Imagination*

Hent de Vries and Samuel Weber, eds., *Religion and Media*

Niklas Luhmann, *Theories of Distinction: Re-Describing the Descriptions of Modernity*, ed. and introd. William Rasch

Johannes Fabian, *Anthropology with an Attitude: Critical Essays*

Michel Henry, *I am the Truth: Toward a Philosophy of Christianity*

Gil Anidjar, *"Our Place in Al-Andalus": Kabbalah, Philosophy, Literature in Arab-Jewish Letters*

Hélène Cixous and Jacques Derrida, *Veils*

F. R. Ankersmit, *Historical Representation*

F. R. Ankersmit, *Political Representation*

Elissa Marder, *Dead Time: Temporal Disorders in the Wake of Modernity (Baudelaire and Flaubert)*

Reinhart Koselleck, *The Practice of Conceptual History: Timing History, Spacing Concepts*

Niklas Luhmann, *The Reality of the Mass Media*

Hubert Damisch, *A Childhood Memory by Piero della Francesca*

Hubert Damisch, *A Theory of /Cloud/: Toward a History of Painting*

Jean-Luc Nancy, *The Speculative Remark: (One of Hegel's bon mots)*

Jean-François Lyotard, *Soundproof Room: Malraux's Anti-Aesthetics*

Jan Patočka, *Plato and Europe*

Hubert Damisch, *Skyline: The Narcissistic City*

Isabel Hoving, *In Praise of New Travelers: Reading Caribbean Migrant Women Writers*

Richard Rand, ed., *Futures: Of Jacques Derrida*

William Rasch, *Niklas Luhmann's Modernity: The Paradoxes of Differentiation*

Jacques Derrida and Anne Dufourmantelle, *Of Hospitality*

Jean-François Lyotard, *The Confession of Augustine*

Kaja Silverman, *World Spectators*

Samuel Weber, *Institution and Interpretation: Expanded Edition*

Jeffrey S. Librett, *The Rhetoric of Cultural Dialogue: Jews and Germans in the Epoch of Emancipation*

Ulrich Baer, *Remnants of Song: Trauma and the Experience of Modernity in Charles Baudelaire and Paul Celan*

Samuel C. Wheeler III, *Deconstruction as Analytic Philosophy*

David S. Ferris, *Silent Urns: Romanticism, Hellenism, Modernity*

Rodolphe Gasché, *Of Minimal Things: Studies on the Notion of Relation*

Sarah Winter, *Freud and the Institution of Psychoanalytic Knowledge*

Samuel Weber, *The Legend of Freud: Expanded Edition*

Aris Fioretos, ed., *The Solid Letter: Readings of Friedrich Hölderlin*

J. Hillis Miller/Manuel Asensi, *Black Holes/J. Hillis Miller; or, Boustrophedonic Reading*

Miryam Sas, *Fault Lines: Cultural Memory and Japanese Surrealism*

Peter Schwenger, *Fantasm and Fiction: On Textual Envisioning*

Didier Maleuvre, *Museum Memories: History, Technology, Art*

Jacques Derrida, *Monolingualism of the Other; or, The Prosthesis of Origin*

Andrew Baruch Wachtel, *Making a Nation, Breaking a Nation: Literature and Cultural Politics in Yugoslavia*

Niklas Luhmann, *Love as Passion: The Codification of Intimacy*

Mieke Bal, ed., *The Practice of Cultural Analysis: Exposing Interdisciplinary Interpretation*

Jacques Derrida and Gianni Vattimo, eds., *Religion*